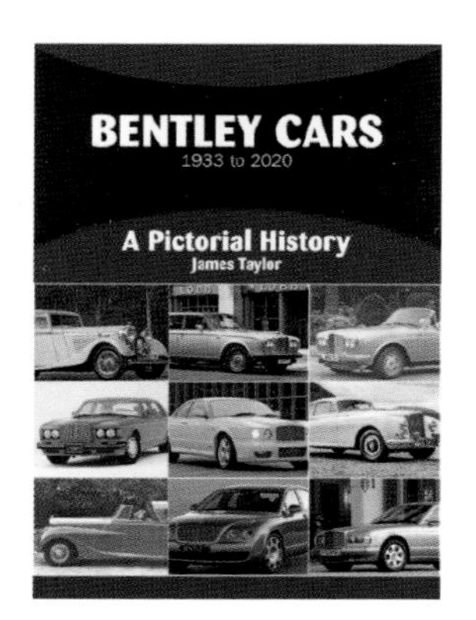
BENTLEY CARS
1933 to 2020
A Pictorial History
James Taylor

T0349421

A Pictorial History **- more titles in this series**

Audi Cars 1968 to 2010 (Alder)
Austin Cars 1948 to 1990 (Rowe)
BMW Cars 1945 to 2013 (Alder)
Citroën Cars 1934 to 1986 (Parish)
Ford Cars – Ford UK cars 1945-1995 (Rowe)
Lotus Cars 1952 to 2024 (Vale)
Jaguar Cars 1946 to 2008 (Thorley)
Mercedes Benz Cars 1947 to 2000 (Taylor)
MG Cars 1930 to 2006 (Alder)
Morris Cars 1948 to 1984 (Newell)
Riley & Wolseley Cars 1948 to 1975 (Rowe)
Rootes Cars of the 50s, 60s & 70s (Hillman, Humber, Singer, Sunbeam & Talbot) (Rowe)
Rover Cars 1945 to 2005 (Taylor)
Saab Cars 1949 to 2011 (Parish)
Triumph & Standard Cars 1945 to 1984 (Warrington)
Vauxhall Cars 1945 to 1995 (Alder)
Volvo Cars 1945 to 1985 (Alder)

More Bentley titles

Bentley Continental, Corniche & Azure (Bennett)
Inside the Rolls-Royce & Bentley Styling Department 1971 to 2001(Hull)
Rolls-Royce Silver Spirit & Silver Spur, Bentley Mulsanne, Eight, Continental, Brooklands & Azure (Bobbitt)
Rolls Royce Silver Shadow/Bentley T-Series, Camargue & Corniche (Bobbitt)
Rolls-Royce Silver Shadow & Bentley T-Series – The Essential Buyer's Guide (Bobbitt)

www.veloce.co.uk

First published in 2025 by Veloce, an imprint of David and Charles Limited. Tel +44 (0)1305 260068 / e-mail info@veloce.co.uk / web www.veloce.co.uk.
ISBN: 9781836440055 Readers with ideas for automotive books, or books on other transport or related hobby subjects, are invited to write to the editorial director of Veloce at the above address. British Library Cataloguing in Publication Data – A catalogue record for this book is available from the British Library. Design and production by Veloce. Printed and bound in the UK by Short Run Press Ltd.

BENTLEY CARS
1933 to 2020

A Pictorial History
James Taylor

CONTENTS

INTRODUCTION

The Bentley marque has become a legend among British motor manufacturers, thanks in no small part to the racing successes of its early days that made it stand out above its contemporaries. Yet its trajectory to the position it enjoys today has by no means been smooth.

Bentley was founded in 1919 by Walter Owen Bentley and delivered its first cars to customers in 1921. The initial model was a sporting type called the 3 Litre after the size of its four-cylinder engine, and, as the 1920s progressed, it was further developed and joined by the 4½ Litre, which eventually replaced it. Meanwhile, a six-cylinder model called the 6½ Litre was made available, and this, too, was developed, in particular, with a higher-performance Speed Six model. The ultimate W O Bentley was an 8-litre model, introduced in 1930.

All these cars were individually bodied, and their variety is too great to include in this book. Their racing successes, especially at Le Mans, and their public esteem were unfortunately not matched by financial success for the company, and a receiver was appointed in 1931. The Bentley company was bought by Rolls-Royce, which determined to use the marque's sporting credibility to broaden the appeal of its own products. The old Bentley works at Cricklewood were closed, and production resumed at Rolls-Royce in Derby in 1933, with new sporting models that shared many components with the more staid luxury cars built by the new parent company.

The Bentley marque held its head high during the 1930s, but production ceased in 1939 as the British motor industry was turned over to war work. When the war ended in 1945, Rolls-Royce moved its car division to the factory at Crewe where it had been building aero engines for the RAF, and with it went the Bentley marque. The new postwar cars presented a very different picture, with standardised bodies pressed from steel rather than built by hand, although the earlier high standards of quality were maintained.

There is more detail about the Bentley models of the 1950s and 1960s in the main body of this book. Suffice to say here that, with the exception of the legendary Continental, Bentleys became a less expensive clone of their Rolls-Royce equivalents. Then, in 1970, development problems with a new Rolls-Royce aero engine caused the collapse of the parent company. In the subsequent reconstruction, the car division was made a separate business, although the Bentley marque was at its lowest ebb in this period, when at one point less than 5 per cent of the cars built at Crewe had Bentley badges.

In 1980, the two marques changed hands yet again when they were bought by the armaments group, Vickers plc. Vickers set about reviving the Bentley marque, giving it a clear performance identity of its own that was exemplified by the Mulsanne Turbo of 1982. The marque was thriving by 1997, when Vickers decided to sell the car side of its business. After a complicated and confusing period in which Rolls-Royce was sold to BMW but Bentley went to the Volkswagen Group, the marque was revitalised with new models in the early 2000s. Now sharing many major components with other VW Group models, the subsequent Bentley models established the name more strongly than ever, and have successfully maintained the elite nature of the Bentley brand while increasing its sales exponentially.

I am very grateful to the press department of Bentley Motors, which has supplied many of the pictures used to illustrate this book. My thanks also go to those generous individuals who have made their work available for reproduction through Wikimedia Commons, and who are credited individually alongside the relevant photographs. The late Bernard L King was also very helpful in supplying pictures.

There are very many books about Bentley cars in print, and some of them have my own name on the cover. The present one can only give an outline of the story, which would need several very large volumes to cover thoroughly. For readers who want to take their interest further, I can only encourage a search on the internet (or, in the old-fashioned way, in a library) to find further enlightenment.

James Taylor

THE DERBY BENTLEYS

In the 1930s, although mass production of car bodies was gradually becoming the norm, it was still customary for the builders of high-class chassis to provide only the chassis; the customer could then choose a body built to their taste by one of the many independent coachbuilders.

W O Bentley, who had founded the marque in 1919, had frequently sighed over the fact that so many customers ordered heavy, luxurious bodywork that reduced the performance of his deliberately sporting chassis, and there was no real change for the Derby Bentleys. Nevertheless, Rolls-Royce did insist on inspecting every car once it had been completed by its coachbuilder, and would not provide a guarantee for any it considered might compromise the established Bentley marque values. This prevented any unpleasant excesses – although not every body approved met the highest standards of contemporary taste.

By the time of the Derby Bentley, closed bodywork was becoming the norm, and most chassis carried such coachwork when new; drop-head coupé and tourer styles accounted for only about 25 per cent of the bodies built. In fact, the most popular style was the sports saloon, which was not particularly sporting but usually had a 'four-light' design (with four side windows), whereas the more formal saloons and limousines typically had a six-light design.

Stylish sports saloons were favoured on the Derby Bentleys, and this one by Hooper for the 1933 Olympia Show was typical.

Even though the general public tended to believe that every coachbuilt body was a bespoke creation, in practice this was far from the case. There certainly were individual designs, but by the time of the 3½-litre Bentley, many coachbuilders had learned how to minimise cost and manufacturing complications by relying on designs they could build in batches. At the start of a new season, typically in the autumn, they would build a prototype of a new design and display it at

This attractive sports saloon body on the 3½-litre chassis was by Thrupp & Maberly.

the London Motor Show (and, sometimes, elsewhere). When orders began to come in, they might anticipate eventual sales of perhaps ten altogether, and might build them all at the same time. Individual variations could be accommodated so the customer could feel they were buying a bespoke body, but in practice this was the nearest that craftsman-built bodies came to volume production.

During the era of the Derby Bentleys, no fewer than 56 different coachbuilders created bodies for chassis that bore the Bentley name when those chassis were new and still in production. The majority were in Britain, but there were also some attractive bodies from coachbuilders on the European continent, especially for customers who lived there. It is also important to remember that body and chassis were not seen as inseparable entities in this period. Several wealthy customers decided to have their cars rebodied after a few years, partly to keep them fresh and fashionable, and partly because (for example) they might have tired of the original saloon and wanted a more frivolous drop-head coupé instead. Though expensive, this was much less costly than buying a completely new car – particularly one that cost as much as a Bentley.

The Yorkshire coachbuilder Rippon bowed to contemporary aerodynamic fashion with this fastback sports saloon.

Barker, the royal coachbuilder, could even make a sports saloon like this one look like a formal body.

The 3½ Litre, 1933-1937

Once Rolls-Royce had acquired the Bentley business, it was clear it had to get a new Bentley model into production as quickly as possible to capitalise on the goodwill that came with the Bentley name. The simplest and most cost-effective way of doing so was to base the new Bentley on work already being done for a possible new, smaller Rolls-Royce under the code name of Peregrine. This had a lightweight chassis with a wheelbase six inches shorter than the contemporary Rolls-Royce 20/25 model, and was a low-slung type well suited to the sort of sporting bodywork expected of a Bentley.

The initial plan to give the Bentley a supercharged version of the Peregrine engine ran into difficulties, and so the Rolls-Royce engineers decided to try a version of the existing six-cylinder 20/25 engine in the Peregrine chassis. The results were immediately satisfying, and Sir Henry Royce gave his approval to proceed with further development towards the end of 1932. Sadly, Royce's health was already failing, and when he died in 1933 he may never have seen any of the new Bentleys beyond the first prototype.

The new Bentley prototypes took on the code name of Bensport. The 3669cc engine was given twin carburettors, a new induction system and a higher compression ratio, and delivered 110bhp on the test bed, or about

This coupé by Gurney Nutting was a very special design. It was called a 'sedanca coupé' when sold by London dealer HR Owen.

There were also a few bodies by overseas coachbuilders on the 3½-litre chassis. This drop-head coupé came from the Parisian firm of Antem.

One of the less well-known coachbuilders was Lancefield, which nevertheless was courageous enough to experiment with a fastback design.

25 per cent more than its parent. The 20/25 gearbox was retained, but with closer gearing to suit the more sporting nature of the Bentley. Brakes were rod-operated and benefited from a gearbox-driven mechanical servo, as used on Rolls-Royce models of the time. This was a speed-sensitive device built under licence from Hispano-Suiza.

The new model was introduced at the autumn 1933 Olympia Show in London as the Bentley 3½ Litre, a name chosen to fit in with previous Bentley practice of naming their cars after the engine size. It was very well received, and no doubt there was a good deal of relief at the Rolls-Royce works in Derby that the somewhat rushed development had not overlooked any concealed problems. The 3½ Litre became the first of the so-called Derby Bentleys, a name so much better suited to them than the motor trade's somewhat disrespectful description of them as Rolls-Bentleys. Rolls-Royce advertised them as the Silent Sports Car, a very neat piece of marketing which encapsulated their appeal very well.

MODELS: 3½ Litre, all with right-hand drive.

Gurney Nutting mastered the pillarless body design, which gave a large, open area when the windows were dropped. They called this a saloon coupé.

ENGINE: 3669cc OHV six-cylinder, twin SU carburettors, 114bhp.
GEARBOX: Four forward speeds, with synchromesh on third and fourth only.
SUSPENSION, STEERING & BRAKES: Semi-elliptic leaf springs front and rear, with hydraulic dampers all round. Manual damper control from chassis B1CW. Worm and nut steering. Drum brakes front and rear, with mechanical servo assistance.
DIMENSIONS: Length: 14ft 6in (4674mm). **Width:** 5ft 9in (1753mm). **Wheelbase:** 10ft 6in (3200mm). **Track:** front and rear, 4ft 8in (1422mm).
PERFORMANCE & FUEL CONSUMPTION: 91mph, 0-60mph in 18-21 sec, 16-18mpg.
PRODUCTION TOTAL: 1177.

The 4¼ Litre, 1936-1939

Despite the acknowledged excellence of the Bentley 3½ Litre, it could not remain the market leader forever. Other makers, such as Alvis and Lagonda, countered with powerful new models which may have lacked the overall refinement of the Bentley but provided similar performance and – most importantly – were considerably less expensive. Lagonda's coup was to secure the services of W O Bentley himself, who had been kicking his heels at Rolls-Royce, where his design and engineering talents were not needed.

The obvious next stage for Bentley was to improve the performance of its cars, and again it was able to draw on work being done for Rolls-Royce models. An enlarged version of the 20/25's six-cylinder engine was being prepared for introduction in 1936 (when it would appear in the 25/30 model), mainly to counter the perennial problem of excessively

The Rolls-Royce company particularly favoured the French coachbuilder Vanvooren, which pioneered pillarless bodies. The advantages are seen in this picture of a saloon on the 4¼-litre Bentley chassis.

heavy coachwork. This had an enlarged bore that raised the swept volume to 4257cc, and was first tried in a Bensport prototype, in February 1936.

Bentley made it available as soon as it could, and by spring 1936 the new '4¼-litre' engine was being offered as an option for an extra £50 over the price of a 3½-litre. The maker described it as an option, to avoid upsetting buyers still awaiting delivery of 3½-litre models, but even then had to adjust production to demand as several chassis that had been laid down as 3½-litre types were fitted with 4¼-litre engines and renumbered in the sequences designated for the new models.

The new and more powerful engine quickly attracted customers and was generally considered to be both excellent and a welcome improvement over the earlier 3½-litre type. All seemed well, until some engines began to suffer from premature bearing wear. It quickly became clear this only occurred when the cars

Park Ward was responsible for the sports saloon body seen here on a 4¼-litre model.

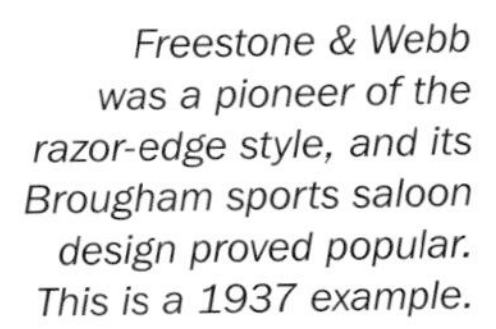

Freestone & Webb was a pioneer of the razor-edge style, and its Brougham sports saloon design proved popular. This is a 1937 example.

Vanden Plas coachwork was particularly elegant, as seen on this drop-head coupé.

Park Ward's idea of a drop-head coupé was less sporting, but no less elegant.

Carlton was a small London coachbuilder, but designs like this one on the 4¼-litre chassis punched above their weight.

were driven flat out for long distances (which mainly occurred on the European continent, as this kind of driving was impossible on British roads). The simplest solution was to modify the gearbox, and so the 1938 models (those of the M series chassis) pioneered a revised four-speed type in which third gear was the direct top and fourth was an overdrive ratio. These later cars also benefited from evolutionary improvements such as lighter steering from a lower-geared Marles steering box and greater ride comfort from larger-section tyres on smaller-diameter wheels.

Many coachbuilders continued to offer the same styles as they had for the 3½-litre cars, although these styles gradually evolved over the years of 4¼-litre chassis production. Nevertheless, the last of the 4¼-litre cars were in most cases readily recognisable as the descendants of the earlier Derby Bentleys.

MODELS: 4¼ Litre (1936-1937), 4¼ Litre with Overdrive (1937-1939). All chassis were built with right-hand drive.
ENGINE: 4257cc OHV six-cylinder, twin SU carburettors, 125bhp.
GEARBOX: Four forward speeds, with synchromesh on third and fourth only, fourth geared as overdrive from chassis B2MR.
SUSPENSION, STEERING & BRAKES: Semi-elliptic leaf springs front and rear, with

This wonderful aerodynamic design was built by the French coachbuilder Pourtout and was the inspiration for the Corniche prototype.

hydraulic dampers all round. Worm and nut steering. Marles cam-and-roller steering from B2MR. Drum brakes front and rear, with mechanical servo assistance.
DIMENSIONS: **Length:** 14ft 6in (4674mm). **Width:** 5ft 9in (1753mm). **Wheelbase:** 10ft 6in (3200mm). **Track:** front and rear, 4ft 8in (1422mm).
PERFORMANCE & FUEL CONSUMPTION: 91-93mph, 0-60mph in 16-17 sec, 16-18mpg.
PRODUCTION TOTAL: 1234.

Bentley Mk V, 1939-1940

Derby's engineers started work on the next new Bentley model during 1937. The prototypes were again numbered in the Bensport series, of which this was the fifth iteration. The internal designation of Bensport V influenced the choice of public model

Representing dashboard design at the start of the 1940s, this is the Park Ward Mk V Sports Saloon. (Tentenths, CC by-SA 3.0)

This very special alloy-panelled Park Ward Sports Saloon on the Mk V chassis was one of the few completed – and that not until 1941. (Tentenths, CC by-SA 3.0)

name, and by the time the car was ready for release it had been given the name of Bentley Mk V. There were also plans for a special high-performance derivative that was to be known as the Corniche; this is dealt with separately here.

However, the Mk V's story was abruptly curtailed by the outbreak of war in September 1939. The London Motor Show planned for Earls Court in October was cancelled, and with it went plans to put the car into volume production. Of the 35 chassis laid down to become the first batch of Mk Vs, it is generally accepted that 18 were scrapped. The remaining 17 were completed as running chassis, and 12 of those were turned into complete cars by coachbuilders Rolls-Royce had selected. Just seven of those 12 cars still survive.

The standard chassis for the new car was developed with the code name of Clipper; other variants were also under development, including an eight-cylinder car, a long-wheelbase chassis and the high-performance type coded as Corniche. There were major differences from the 4¼-litre type, of which the most profound was the replacement of the beam front axle with an independent system related to that developed for the Rolls-Royce Wraith. This allowed the engine to be mounted further forward in the chassis, which allowed additional room in the body. The chassis frame had very deep side

Another Park Ward Sports Saloon on the Mk V chassis nevertheless has some differences from the one shown above. Side-mounted spare wheels were very much of their time. (Vauxford CCA-SA 4.0)

rails, to absorb the stresses of the new front suspension and to improve refinement and handling.

The radiator and grille were also mounted further forward, giving a very different side profile. Smaller (16in) wheels further altered the proportions; one prototype had wire wheels and these were shown in the sales catalogue produced for the Mk V, but disc wheels were becoming the norm and were used on the other known cars.

Proceeding in small increments, as was the Rolls-Royce way, the engineers planned to use a revised 4¼-litre engine, derived from the one in the latest Rolls-Royce Wraith. The four-speed gearbox was also further developed with the addition of synchromesh to second gear, leaving only bottom gear unsynchronised.

Prototype Bentley Mk V cars began long-distance testing on the European continent during 1938. These had bodies by Park Ward, the coachbuilder partly owned by Rolls-Royce since 1933, and among them was a new sports saloon style intended to become one of the recommended standard types. However, several of the initial production chassis were sent to other favoured coachbuilders in anticipation of having as wide a variety of options as possible on display at the 1939 Motor Show. Of the ten cars intended for the show, only one was completed – a six-light saloon by H J Mulliner.

MODEL: Mk V.
ENGINE: 4257cc OHV six-cylinder, twin SU carburettors, 125bhp.
GEARBOX: Four forward speeds, with synchromesh on second, third and fourth only, fourth geared as overdrive.
SUSPENSION, STEERING & BRAKES: Independent front suspension with coil springs, wishbones and anti-roll bar, rear suspension with semi-elliptic leaf springs on 'live' axle, hydraulic dampers all round, with manual control at the rear. Marles cam-and-roller steering. Drum brakes front and rear, with mechanical servo assistance.
DIMENSIONS: Length: 15ft 11in (4851mm). **Width:** 5ft 9in (1753mm). **Wheelbase:** 10ft 4in (3150mm). **Track:** front, 4ft 8¼in (1428mm), rear, 4ft 10in (1473mm).
PERFORMANCE & FUEL CONSUMPTION: "Close to 100mph" according to the manufacturer's tests. Fuel consumption estimated by *The Motor* at 16-20mpg.
PRODUCTION TOTAL: 12 (but see text).

The Corniche, 1939

The Bentley Corniche was planned as a high-performance derivative of the Mk V, and was scheduled for introduction a year after the parent saloon. Whether it would have been called Corniche in production is unclear, because that name was actually the development code for the car.

Its extra performance came from larger carburettors and a higher compression ratio, a taller axle ratio and lightweight and aerodynamic coachwork. French coachbuilder Carrosserie Vanvooren constructed a streamlined four-door pillarless sports saloon

The Corniche prototype had a lightweight aerodynamic body on a Mk V chassis, and a tuned engine as well. This is the magnificent reconstruction built by Bentley Motors.

The Corniche still looks striking and immensely stylish more than 80 years after it was designed.

for the sole prototype chassis (14-B-V). Its design, by Georges Paulin, incorporated a streamlined nose without the traditional Bentley radiator grille.

The Corniche prototype was seriously damaged in a rollover accident during testing in France in early August 1939. The body was removed and sent for repair at a local coachworks, and the chassis was returned to Crewe for repairs. The Second World War began in September 1939, and the repaired body was waiting on the dockside at Dieppe when it was destroyed in a bombing raid. Due to the war, no further work was done on the Corniche.

Nevertheless, the Corniche created its own legend and, in 2001, former Bentley director Ken Lea initiated a project to recreate the car around parts that had been manufactured for the original first production batch. A team of volunteers managed to put the chassis together and, in 2008, Bentley Motors provided an injection of funds to enable the body to be built. Using outline drawings created by the original designer, Paulin, the body was built to the original specifications, initially by a small specialist coachbuilder and subsequently by Bentley's Mulliner bespoke division at Crewe. The recreated car was revealed during 2019 as part of Bentley's centenary celebrations.

MODEL: Corniche sports saloon (prototype only).
ENGINE: 4257cc OHV six-cylinder, twin SU carburettors, 142bhp.
GEARBOX: Four forward speeds, with synchromesh on second, third and fourth only, fourth geared as overdrive.
SUSPENSION, STEERING & BRAKES: Independent front suspension with coil springs, wishbones and anti-roll bar, rear suspension with semi-elliptic leaf springs on 'live' axle, hydraulic dampers all round, with manual control at the rear. Marles cam-and-roller steering. Drum brakes front and rear, with mechanical servo assistance.
DIMENSIONS: Length: 15ft 11in (4851mm). **Width:** 5ft 9in (1753mm). **Wheelbase:** 10ft 4in (3150mm). **Track:** front, 4ft 8¼in (1428mm), rear, 4ft 10in (1473mm).
PERFORMANCE & FUEL CONSUMPTION: Bentley's own test figures showed a 110mph top speed.
PRODUCTION TOTAL: 1 (plus a modern replica).

The Corniche dashboard was a state-of-the-art design; even the heater (the round box below it) was an advanced feature in 1939.

MK VI AND R TYPE

The postwar rationalised range of cars from Crewe was carefully planned with as much common engineering as possible between Bentley and Rolls-Royce models while preserving the individual status of each. There was also a new reliance on 'standard steel' bodies – built by Pressed Steel rather than by the traditional coachbuilders. Bare chassis remained available for custom coachwork, but the number of independent coachbuilders was shrinking in this period and would shrink further, largely due to the change of policy at Crewe.

This 1951 Mk VI has the standard steel body, which reflected ideas pioneered on the prewar Mk V. Rear-wheel spats were fashionable at the time. (Charles01/Free GNU Doc Licence)

The Mk VI, 1946-1952

Although the 4.25-litre six-cylinder engine used in the Bentley Mk VI was the same as that in the Rolls-Royce Silver Wraith, it was in a different state of tune. The Bentley chassis was also shorter, and while the Rolls-Royce was sold as a bare chassis for traditional hand-built coachwork, the Bentley was sold primarily as a complete car with a standard saloon body manufactured by Pressed Steel. There would be coachbuilt Bentleys too, but they would account for only about 19 per cent of the chassis produced.

The Bentley Mk VI had a twin-carburettor version of the six-cylinder engine, and its standard four-door body was designed in the sports saloon idiom, as a four-light type. Though sporting by the standards of the day, with a 93mph top speed, it was also cautiously conservative, with separate front wings and overall lines that embodied some elements of the prewar razor-edge style. The four-speed gearbox had a traditional right-hand change outboard of the driver, and the chassis incorporated a centralised lubrication system, while the brakes were a hybrid system with hydraulic actuation at the front but rod operation at the rear. They were supplemented by the traditional Rolls-Royce friction disc servo.

The Bentley name was not well known in the US so, to achieve sales there, Rolls-Royce had to make available a version of the Mk VI with its own badges. This materialised in April 1949 as the Rolls-Royce Silver Dawn, but at this stage it was strictly for export only and had a lower state of tune than the Mk VI. Then in 1951, a big-bore, 4.5-litre six-cylinder engine replaced the original 4.25-litre and brought

H J Mulliner's idea of a saloon body for the Mk VI chassis featured even deeper rear-wheel spats. This is a 1949 car.

The sedanca coupé was rare in the postwar years, but coachbuilder Gurney Nutting designed this beautiful 'teardrop' style.

100mph performance within reach for the first time. The Bentley Mk VI gave way to the visually very similar R Type in 1952. Coachbuilt cars were predominantly saloon styles but other, less numerous types included drop-head coupés and sedanca de ville styles. The largest numbers of coachbuilt Mk VI Bentleys were bodied by H J Mulliner, James Young, Park Ward, and Freestone & Webb, but many other companies built such cars in penny numbers.

MODELS: Mk VI 4.25-litre, Mk VI 4.5-litre.
ENGINE: 4257cc OHV six-cylinder, twin SU carburettors, approx 125bhp (1946-1951), 4566cc OHV six-cylinder, twin SU carburettors, approx 150bhp (1951-1952).
GEARBOX: Four forward speeds, with synchromesh on second, third and fourth only.
SUSPENSION, STEERING & BRAKES: Independent front suspension with coil springs, wishbones and anti-roll bar, rear suspension with semi-elliptic leaf springs on 'live' axle, hydraulic dampers all round, with manual control at the rear. Marles cam-and-roller steering. Drum brakes front and rear, with mechanical servo assistance; hydraulic operation at the front and mechanical operation at the rear.
DIMENSIONS: **Length:** 15ft 11½in to 16ft 4½in (4864mm to 4991mm), depending on bumpers fitted. **Width:** standard saloon,

H J Mulliner drew up this curvaceous saloon style, hinting at shapes to come, but the spats were again very much of their time. (boybentley, CCA 2.0)

Again, bodies by overseas coachbuilders were rare, but this one by the Italian Pininfarina company in 1949 was a triumph.(Rex Gray, CC2.0 Generic)

5ft 9in (1753mm). **Height:** standard saloon, 5ft 4.5in (1638mm). **Wheelbase:** 10ft 0in (3048mm). **Track:** front, 4ft 8½in (1435mm), rear, 4ft 10½in (1486mm).
PERFORMANCE & FUEL CONSUMPTION: 93mph, 0-60mph in 15.2 sec, 16-17mpg (4.25-litre models). 100mph, 0-60mph in 15.0 sec, 16mpg (4.5-litre models).
PRODUCTION TOTAL: 5202 (4188 with standard saloon body).

R Type, 1952-1955

A process of constant development at Crewe led to a more major revision of the Bentley Mk VI in 1952. Known during development as the B7 (Bentley Mk VII), the car was given the more ambiguous and grand-sounding name of R Type for public consumption. The letter was simply the initial code letter of the chassis sequence with which the new model began, but it would set a precedent for later models: the next new Bentley would be known as the S Type, and the T Series would follow.

The major development for the R Type was a longer tail. Many coachbuilders which had worked on the Mk VI chassis had extended its rear to support a longer boot and, for the standard saloon version of the R Type, the extended chassis also brought a larger boot that was blended carefully into the lines of the existing Pressed Steel body.

The R Type of course inherited the 4.5-litre engine from the last of its Mk VI predecessors.

The longer tail of the R Type allowed a larger boot, although the rest of the design remained largely unaltered.

Rear-wheel spats were no longer in fashion by the time of the R Type. This is a 1953 standard saloon, with an elegant two-colour finish. (Anton von Luijk, CCA 2.0)

The four-speed manual gearbox remained standard but a four-speed automatic became available during 1952 for export cars and during 1953 for home market cars. This was a Rolls-Royce adaptation of a General Motors design and was driven through a fluid coupling.

There were still special designs from the coachbuilders: Park Ward bodied this R Type as a drop-head coupé for J D Rockefeller in 1954.(Sicnag, CCA 2.0)

H J Mulliner's lightweight sports saloon heralded a new era of sweeping wing lines. This is a 1953 R Type.

A further important development during 1953 was a change from hand-riveted chassis frames to fully welded chassis frames.

Bare chassis were supplied to coachbuilders at customer request, but there were far fewer examples of the R Type than there had been of the Mk VI, and coachbuilt R Types accounted for only about 12 per cent of the total chassis built. Again, the coachbuilders which constructed the largest numbers were H J Mulliner, James Young, Park Ward, Freestone & Webb, and Hooper.

MODELS: R Type, R Type automatic.
ENGINE: 4566cc OHV six-cylinder, twin SU carburettors, approx 150bhp.
GEARBOX: Four forward speeds, with synchromesh on second, third and fourth only. Optional four-speed automatic with fluid coupling.
SUSPENSION, STEERING & BRAKES: Independent front suspension with coil springs, wishbones and anti-roll bar, rear suspension with semi-elliptic leaf springs on 'live' axle, hydraulic dampers all round, with manual control at the rear. Marles cam-and-roller steering. Drum brakes front and rear, with mechanical servo assistance, hydraulic operation at the front and mechanical operation at the rear.
DIMENSIONS: Length: 16ft 7½in to 17ft 6in (5067mm to 5334mm), depending on bumpers fitted. **Width:** standard saloon, 5ft 9in (1753mm). **Height:** standard saloon, 5ft 4.5in (1638mm). **Wheelbase:** 10ft 0in (3048mm). **Track:** front, 4ft 8½in (1435mm), rear, 4ft 10½in (1486mm).

Inspired by a less resolved Hooper design, Freestone & Webb came up with this most elegant style that would outlast the R Type chassis. (K-J Rossfeldt)

PERFORMANCE & FUEL CONSUMPTION: 100mph, 0-60mph in 15.0 sec, 16mpg.
PRODUCTION TOTAL: 2322 (2037 with standard saloon body).

R Type Continental, 1952-1955

The R Type Continental was the glamorous and legendary realisation of ideas tried just before the war with the Bentley Corniche prototype based on the Bentley Mk V chassis. The Continental name had a certain currency from its use for the Rolls-Royce Phantom Continental chassis of the 1920s and 1930s. Like those cars, the Bentley was designed as a high-speed, long-distance touring car that would be particularly suitable for the unrestricted roads on the European continent.

The early cars were actually based on the Bentley Mk VI chassis with the 4.5-litre twin-carburettor engine and were simply known as Bentley Continental types; the R Type name was added later. Their chassis had the standard 120in wheelbase but was endowed with taller gearing and other modifications to enhance performance. Central to the concept of the Continental were weight saving and aerodynamics, and in the beginning the cars were available only with a lightweight aluminium-panelled two-door fastback saloon body designed at Rolls-Royce and constructed

The fastback design of the 'standard' Continental body is clear here; some of the later examples dispensed with the wheel spats, which were going out of fashion by about 1954.

The dashboard of a 1954 LHD R Type Continental shows the big steering wheel and the floor-mounted gearchange, which was outboard of the driver on RHD cars. (Rex Gray, CCA 2.0)

This 1955 R Type Continental was the supercar of its day, and a supremely elegant design as well. (Tony Hisgett/CCA 2.0 Generic)

Park Ward also offered a style for the Continental, and one that more closely anticipated future design trends.

by the coachbuilder H J Mulliner. In this form, the car was capable of 115mph, a speed that was in the realms of fantasy when the Continental became available in 1952, and which made it into the world's fastest production four-seater.

The Continental was always hugely expensive and, in original form with the Mulliner fastback body, was an exceptionally attractive design with enormous presence. Crewe eventually acceded to demands for bare chassis to be bodied by other coachbuilders, but insisted that only two-door coachwork should be constructed. Inevitably, the original lightweight, high-performance nature of the Continental became a little blurred over time as customers ordered weighty items such as stronger bumpers, more comfortably padded seats and other equipment that had not been part of the original concept.

Partly to counter these issues, the six-cylinder engine was bored out once again to 4.9 litres in 1954, and in this form was used in the last two series of the Bentley Continental chassis. This engine was also destined for use in the Rolls-Royce and Bentley models that would replace the R Type in 1955.

Of the 208 R Type Continental chassis built, no fewer than 193 had the factory-designed fastback bodywork. The other 15 were bodied by Park Ward in Britain, Franay in France, Graber in Switzerland and Pininfarina in Italy.

MODELS: Continental 4.5-litre, Continental 4.9-litre.

ENGINE: 4566cc six-cylinder, twin SU carburettors, approx 153bhp (1952-1954), 4887cc six-cylinder, twin SU carburettors, approx 155bhp (1954-1955).

GEARBOX: Four forward speeds, with synchromesh on second, third and fourth only. Optional four-speed automatic with fluid coupling.

SUSPENSION, STEERING & BRAKES: Independent front suspension with coil springs, wishbones and anti-roll bar, rear suspension with semi-elliptic leaf springs on 'live' axle, hydraulic dampers all round, with manual control at the rear. Marles cam-and-roller steering. Drum brakes front and rear, with mechanical servo assistance, hydraulic operation at the front and mechanical operation at the rear.

DIMENSIONS: Length: depending on bumpers fitted, 17ft 2½in to 17ft 7½in (5245mm to 5372mm). **Width:** standard fastback saloon, 5ft 10in (1778mm). **Height:** standard fastback saloon, 5ft 3in (1600mm). **Wheelbase:** 10ft 0in (3048mm).

PERFORMANCE & FUEL CONSUMPTION: 120mph, 0-60mph in 13.5 sec, 16-21mpg (typical).

PRODUCTION TOTAL: 208.

There was a drop-head coupé version of the Park Ward style for the Continental, too. (Anton von Luijk CCA 2.0)

THE S TYPE

For the next generation of cars planned to succeed the R Type and its Rolls-Royce Silver Dawn equivalent, Crewe planned to use the latest 4.9-litre engine (as seen in the later R Type Continental), to make the automatic gearbox standard, and to improve interior space. These cars were announced in 1955 as the Bentley S Type (the name a logical follow-up to the R Type) and the Rolls-Royce Silver Cloud. In saloon form, they were identical in all but radiator grille and marque identification.

Monocoque construction was still some time in the future for Crewe, and the cars retained a separate chassis. As with the R Type, there was a 'standard steel' saloon body, but the chassis was also made available for coachbuilt bodies, and there was a special Continental derivative intended to give the Bentley marque its own distinctive model.

The S Type went through three phases in a long production career that lasted until 1965. The first cars, retrospectively S1 types, had the six-cylinder engine. From 1959 there was a new V8 engine, which created the S2 models and, in further modified form from 1962, the final S3 types. There were Continental derivatives of all three.

S1, 1955-1959

The S1 was much the same size as the R Type that it replaced, but it looked larger thanks to its less upright lines, and had an extra three inches in the wheelbase to provide more room within the body. The 'standard steel' body was designed by John Blatchley at Crewe and built by Pressed Steel. It was well received. Extraordinarily well-proportioned, sleeker than its predecessors and yet still graceful and elegant, it had a presence that remains undeniable 70 years later.

These standard bodies accounted for the lion's share of S1 production, but there were bare chassis available for coachbuilders in the usual way. However, bespoke coachbuilding was in terminal decline by the middle of the 1950s, and in practice many of the coachbuilt bodies came from Rolls-Royce-owned Park Ward or from H J Mulliner, which would also be taken over by Rolls-Royce in the early 1960s. A few chassis were bodied by coachbuilders outside Britain, too.

Improvements and changes were introduced gradually. A key year was 1957, when the engine output was increased slightly and a long-wheelbase chassis introduced. The body was extended to suit and, at first glance, it was hard to distinguish from the

The standard saloon was an extremely well-proportioned design that largely obviated the need for coachbuilt alternatives.

Some coachbuilt designs were modified and carried over from those on the R Type chassis. This Freestone & Webb design was one. (Bill Wolf)

standard saloon whose lines it followed very closely. The extra four inches inserted behind the centre door pillar barely affected the styling, but did turn the S1 into an entirely credible limousine, and some were fitted with divisions. However, the long-wheelbase Bentley remained much rarer than its Rolls-Royce counterpart, and only 35 were built on the S1 chassis.

MODELS: Standard saloon, long-wheelbase saloon, bare chassis for coachbuilders.
ENGINE: 4887cc OHV six-cylinder, twin SU carburettors, 175bhp.
GEARBOX: Four-speed GM Hydramatic automatic with fluid coupling.
SUSPENSION, STEERING & BRAKES: Independent front suspension with coil springs, wishbones and anti-roll bar, rear suspension with semi-elliptic leaf springs on 'live' axle, hydraulic dampers all round, with manual control at the rear. Cam-and-roller steering with optional power assistance from late B series, standard on long-wheelbase models. Drum brakes front and rear, hydraulic at the front and hydro-mechanical at the rear, mechanical servo, duplicated front hydraulic circuits from B245BC and on all long-wheelbase chassis.
DIMENSIONS: Length: standard cars, 17ft 8in (5385mm), long wheelbase, 17ft 11¾in (5480mm). **Width:** 6ft 2¾in

Coachbuilder James Young's four-door saloon for the S Type chassis had subtly different lines from those of the standard saloon.

(1898mm). **Height:** standard saloon, 5ft 4in (1625mm). **Wheelbase:** standard saloon, 10ft 3in (3124mm), long wheelbase, 10ft 7in (3226mm).
PERFORMANCE & FUEL CONSUMPTION: 101mph, 0-60mph in 14.2 sec, 13-16mpg.
PRODUCTION TOTALS: 3072 (standard wheelbase), 35 (long wheelbase).

S1 Continental, 1955-1959

The R Type Continental did so much to re-establish the glamour associated with the Bentley name in earlier years that it was obvious there should be a Continental derivative of the new S Type chassis. Prototypes were running in 1955 and

Park Ward's beautifully balanced coupé for the Continental was briefly available with fashionable 'fins' on the rear wings. This is a 1956 car.

The H J Mulliner fastback body for the Continental chassis was another carry-over, but always looked heavier than in its original R Type form.

From the front, the revised fastback design looked more modern than the original.

the Bentley Continental S Type entered production in 1956.

The S Type Continental chassis was fundamentally the same as that of the related saloons, but it was fitted with a more powerful development of the 4.9-litre engine, with a taller final drive ratio to enable sustained high-speed running, and with narrower tyres. Crewe anticipated demand for a manual gearbox and made available the type used on the earlier Continental, but it attracted only about 16 orders and was withdrawn in 1957. Power-assisted steering was initially an option, but became standard during 1958.

A limited supply of chassis became available for special coachwork, but, from the beginning, three 'standard' body styles were catalogued. H J Mulliner's all-alloy fastback coupé was derived from the similar style on the R Type Continental, and proved to be the strongest seller. Alongside it, Park Ward offered fixed-head and drop-head coupé versions of a single design, in each case with a conventional projecting luggage boot of good size.

From 1957, H J Mulliner added a four-door sports saloon style called the Flying Spur (after a heraldic symbol), but to gain permission it had to lobby Rolls-Royce management, which was initially unwilling to allow the Continental name to be used on a four-door model. The most numerous special bodies came from James Young; Hooper had a rather uncomfortable and self-consciously modern style; and Franay in France and Graber in Switzerland built one each. Characteristic of all Continentals, whether with standard or special bodies, was a dashboard quite different from that of the standard saloons and incorporating a rev counter.

The Flying Spur was the first four-door design on the Continental chassis and was a major success.

Gradual development of the 4.9-litre engine allowed performance to keep up with the increasingly heavy and luxurious bodies customers wanted, and from autumn 1956 there was a notable increase in the power output. From January 1957, the Z-shaped axle control rod was modified to delete its anti-roll function (a change not introduced on saloons until the S2 types in 1959), and in summer 1958 the centralised chassis lubrication system was deleted.

MODELS: Fastback coupé, fixed-head coupé, drop-head coupé, Flying Spur, chassis for coachbuilders.

This rear view shows how the 'fins' of the Park Ward Continental body were toned down and integrated into the overall design. Two-tone paint schemes like this were common. (H R Owen)

The Hooper design for the Continental chassis did not attract much custom.

ENGINE: 4887cc OHV six-cylinder, twin SU carburettors, 175-180bhp.
GEARBOX: Four-speed GM Hydramatic automatic with fluid coupling (a few special orders with manual gearbox).
SUSPENSION, STEERING & BRAKES: Independent front suspension with coil springs, wishbones and anti-roll bar, rear

The Park Ward design for the Continental chassis worked equally well in drop-head coupé form.

suspension with semi-elliptic leaf springs on 'live' axle, hydraulic dampers all round, with manual control at the rear. Cam-and-roller steering, power assistance initially optional, and standard from 1958. Drum brakes front and rear, hydraulic at the front and hydro-mechanical at the rear, mechanical servo, duplicated front hydraulic circuits from 1956.
DIMENSIONS: **Length:** 17ft 8in (5385mm). **Width:** 6ft 2¾ in (1898mm). **Height:** dependent on body fitted. **Wheelbase:** 10ft 3in (3124mm). **Track:** front, 4ft 10in (1473mm), rear, 5ft 0in (1524mm).
PERFORMANCE & FUEL CONSUMPTION: 115-120mph, 0-60mph in 10.2-12.8 sec, 14.0-15.2mpg.
PRODUCTION TOTAL: 431.

S2, 1959-1962

There was no reason to alter the appearance of the S Type by the end of the 1950s, and Crewe chose not to. However, the introduction of a new and more powerful V8 engine in 1959 was a major change that earned the revised cars the designation of S2 (the Rolls-Royce equivalent was called a Silver Cloud II).

Work had begun on the new engine in 1953 when it became clear that the six-cylinder had reached the limit of its development potential with the 4.9-litre version. A V8 layout was chosen mainly because V8s were becoming almost standard in cars of all types in the US, where Crewe needed to maintain sales. The new engine was designed to fit under the narrow bonnet of the S Type and Silver Cloud models and was made from aluminium alloy to keep its weight down. So successful was this that it actually weighed 30lb less than the six-cylinder it replaced while delivering around 25 per cent more power. Locked into its design was considerable development potential, and the engine would remain in production – albeit through several quite major modifications – for more than 40 years.

The standard Bentley S2 was visually

Like their six-cylinder predecessors, the S2 cars were built on a sturdy separate chassis frame.

The new V8 engine, introduced for the S2 in 1959, inevitably drew on American practice, but was built to the refinement standards set by Rolls-Royce.

Left: The standard S2 saloon was indistinguishable from the six-cylinder S Type from this angle.
Below: The rear view shows the all-red tail lights and special number-plate mounting used on cars for the US. (Mr. choppers/WikiMedia Commons)

almost indistinguishable from its six-cylinder predecessor, although a close look revealed that its headlamps now had plain lenses without the vertical bar and the central 'B' motif of the earlier cars. It was also, of course, essentially the same as its Rolls-Royce counterpart except for badges and the Bentley grille. On the inside, though, subtle changes to the dashboard layout included new face-level adjustable air vents, and there was a column stalk for the indicators instead of the earlier switch on the capping rail. The steering wheel was also smaller in diameter and had a thinner rim.

There were long-wheelbase models alongside the standard saloons and a Continental chassis variant that is described below. Some chassis were made available for bespoke coachwork. Production changes included the introduction of safety belts as an option in 1961, some further small dashboard changes and minor lighting modifications in 1962.

MODELS: Standard saloon, long-wheelbase saloon, bare chassis for coachbuilders.
ENGINE: 6230cc OHV V8, twin SU carburettors, 200bhp (estimated).
GEARBOX: Four-speed GM Hydramatic automatic with fluid coupling.
SUSPENSION, STEERING & BRAKES: Independent front suspension with coil springs, wishbones and anti-roll bar, rear suspension with semi-elliptic leaf springs on 'live' axle, hydraulic dampers all round, with manual control at the rear. Cam-and-roller steering with hydraulic power assistance. Drum brakes front and rear, hydraulic at the front and hydro-

mechanical at the rear, mechanical servo.
DIMENSIONS: **Length:** standard cars, 17ft 8in (5385mm), long wheelbase, 18ft 0in (5486mm). **Width:** 6ft 2¾ in (1898mm). **Height:** standard saloon, 5ft 4in (1625mm). **Wheelbase:** standard cars, 10ft 3in (3124mm), long wheelbase, 10ft 7in (3226mm). **Track:** front, 4ft 10½in (1486mm), rear, 5ft 0in (1524mm).
PERFORMANCE & FUEL CONSUMPTION: 113mph, 0-60mph in 12.6 sec, 11-12mpg.
PRODUCTION TOTALS: 1863 (standard wheelbase), 57 (long wheelbase).

As this side view shows, two-tone Bentleys had the bonnet panels in the lower colour; on the Rolls-Royce equivalent, they were in the upper colour.

S2 Continental, 1959-1962

The Continental was the model that gave Bentley its identity in the 1950s, when a four-door S Type saloon was the same thing as a Rolls-Royce four-door saloon but with a different radiator grille. That remained the case when the S2 Continental was released in 1959, but over the years the distinctive Continental features gradually began to disappear.

In the beginning, the S2 Continental chassis was fundamentally the same as that of the contemporary S2 saloon, but had a taller final drive for more relaxed high-speed cruising, and narrower tyres. It also had uprated front brakes with a four-shoe system. Its steering column was more raked than the saloon type, and its scuttle two inches lower to match. Its radiator grille was both shorter than its saloon counterpart and mounted three inches further forward with a gentle forward slope. This ensured that the Continental would always have a 'long-bonnet' look, and that the bonnet would slope gently downwards to give a subtle impression of additional streamlining.

Nevertheless, the V8 engine had the same state of tune as its saloon counterpart, and standard power steering and air-conditioning emphasised the luxury rather than the performance aspects of the car. It was a specification that required no major changes in three years of production, but from the beginning the lower final drive of the S2 saloons was made optional, emphasising acceleration at the expense of top speed. It was well liked and became standard in summer 1961, so removing another one of the Continental's unique features.

All four of the major coachbuilders were invited to submit designs for the S2 Continental, but the one from Hooper (closely related to its designs for the six-cylinder Continental) was confined to one 1959 chassis. It was the last body the coachbuilder made before closing down. H J Mulliner and Park Ward were initially separate but, in 1961, merged to become Mulliner, Park Ward Ltd, when the operations of both companies were centralised at the former Park Ward factory in Willesden. James Young remained independent, but built only 41 bodies on the S2 Continental chassis.

The initial policy, broadly speaking, was that H J Mulliner would build the closed bodies and that Park Ward would build the drop-head types. H J Mulliner's designs were both carried over from the earlier Continentals, with an updated two-door based on the booted Continental Special introduced in 1958, and the much-admired four-door Flying Spur. The James Young designs were also derivatives of that company's bodies for the six-cylinder Continentals. However, Park Ward's drop-head was startlingly new, with straight-through wing lines penned by a young Norwegian industrial designer called Vilhelm Koren. Its aircraft-type welded steel construction also broke new ground, and it came as standard with an electro-hydraulic operating system for its convertible roof.

MODELS: Fixed-head coupé, drop-head coupé, Flying Spur, chassis for coachbuilders.
ENGINE: 6230cccc V8, twin SU carburettors, 200-220bhp (estimated).
GEARBOX: Four-speed GM Hydramatic automatic with fluid coupling.
SUSPENSION, STEERING & BRAKES: Independent front suspension with coil springs, wishbones and anti-roll bar, rear suspension with semi-elliptic leaf springs on 'live' axle, hydraulic dampers all round, with manual control at the rear. Cam-and-roller steering with hydraulic power assistance. Drum brakes front and rear, hydraulic at the front and hydro-mechanical at the rear, mechanical servo.
DIMENSIONS: Length: 17ft 8in (5385mm). **Width:** 6ft 2¾in (1898mm). **Height:**

The Flying Spur four-door remained available for the S2 Continental.

Luxury, 1960s style, is exemplified by the interior of a LHD S2 Continental Flying Spur.

dependent on bodywork fitted. **Wheelbase:** 10ft 3in (3124mm). **Track:** front, 4ft 10½in (1486mm), rear 5ft 0in (1524mm).
PERFORMANCE & FUEL CONSUMPTION: 115mph, 0-60mph in 12.1 sec, 13mpg.
PRODUCTION TOTAL: 388.

S3, 1962-1965

The Bentley S3 was introduced at the Earls Court Motor Show in October 1962 and was the final update for the S Type range. The chassis was unchanged, but the engine now had larger carburettors and a raised compression ratio (except on some export models), which gave a claimed 7 per cent power increase and slightly improved acceleration. The power assistance was also recalibrated to make the steering lighter at parking speeds.

Front-end changes distinguished the S3 models, most obviously the new paired headlamps.

The most obvious visual change was at the front, where paired headlamps and combined indicator and sidelight units were matched to a shorter radiator grille and a more raked bonnet line. Smaller bumper over-riders were fitted for most markets, and larger tail lamp units now incorporated an amber turn indicator section. Very early cars had no badge on the boot lid, but by December 1962 a simple 'S3' identifier was standard.

Inside the passenger compartment, the biggest change was to individual front seats in place of the earlier split-squab bench. A more upright rear seat squab with slimmer corner padding increased both legroom and seat width. The dashboard capping rail was also changed to incorporate black crash padding.

There were very few changes during production. Stainless steel wheel trims replaced chromed brass in April 1963, and a small B logo was added to the headlamp surrounds in March 1964. From May 1964, wider rear wheel rims were fitted to improve stability at speed; the front wheels retained their original rims.

Long-wheelbase models remained available alongside the standard models, and in theory the S3 chassis was still available for coachbuilt bodies. In practice, however, only one was built (by the Mulliner, Park Ward division). Buyers who wanted a coachbuilt Bentley were steered towards the S3 Continental, and from mid-1964 many were tempted by the newly available version of the

Rolls-Royce Silver Cloud III chassis with a Continental-style raked steering column and lowered scuttle.

These and the S3 Continental models would be the last separate-chassis Bentley cars to be built, and their production ended in mid-1965.

MODELS: Standard saloon, long-wheelbase saloon, bare chassis for coachbuilders.
ENGINE: 6230cc OHV V8, twin SU carburettors, 215-235bhp (estimated).
GEARBOX: Four-speed GM Hydramatic automatic with fluid coupling.
SUSPENSION, STEERING & BRAKES: Independent front suspension with coil springs, wishbones and anti-roll bar, rear suspension with semi-elliptic leaf springs on 'live' axle, hydraulic dampers all round, with manual control at the rear. Cam-and-roller steering with hydraulic power assistance. Drum brakes front and rear, hydraulic at the front and hydro-mechanical at the rear, mechanical servo.
DIMENSIONS: Length: standard cars, 17ft 8in (5385mm), long wheelbase, 18ft 0in (5486mm). **Width:** 6ft 2¾in (1898mm). **Height:** standard saloon, 5ft 4in (1625mm). **Wheelbase:** standard cars, 10ft 3in (3124mm), long wheelbase, 10ft 7in (3226mm). **Track:** front, 4ft 10½in (1486mm), rear, 5ft 0in (1524mm).
PERFORMANCE & FUEL CONSUMPTION: 114-117mph, 0-60mph in 10.1-10.8 sec, 12.3-14.1mpg.
PRODUCTION TOTALS: 1286 (standard wheelbase), 32 (long wheelbase).

S3 Continental, 1962-1965

The S3 Continental chassis announced alongside the new Bentley S3 models in 1962 was very much that of the equivalent saloon. It had the same axle gearing, the same improved power assistance for the steering and the same new distributor and 2in HD8 carburettors. The features that now made it a Continental were its relocated radiator grille, its lower scuttle, and the rev counter that always figured among the instruments. When Rolls-Royce introduced a special version of the Silver Cloud III chassis in 1964, with the same low scuttle and raked steering column as the Continental, the Bentley was left with only its badges and its rev counter to make it special.

There were few production changes to the S3 Continental chassis during its three-year production run, and the only one of real note was that the special four-shoe front brakes were abandoned in summer 1963 in favour of the standard twin-shoe front brakes of the saloons. It was one more change that made the Bentley Continental less special.

Nevertheless, coachbuilt bodywork upheld the uniqueness of the Continental. From the beginning, H J Mulliner offered versions of the much-liked two-door and four-door Flying Spur designs with the new four-lamp front end. Park Ward had the Koren-designed drop-head coupé and matched this with a stunning fixed-head version designed at the same time but sidelined in favour of the H J Mulliner design. From 1963, it actually replaced the H J Mulliner two-door, which went

The Koren drop-head body had been introduced for the S2 Continental and is seen here on an S3 Continental with the paired headlamps.

For the S3, the Koren drop-head was joined by an equally elegant fixed-head coupé. Most were finished in a single colour rather than the two-tone scheme seen here.

out of production. When fitted with the paired headlamps of the S3 range, the Koren designs became universally known as 'Chinese Eye' types because the paired lamps were set at an angle. The fixed-head version in fact became the best-selling body for the S3 Continental.

James Young also adapted its existing designs for the Continental chassis to take the latest paired headlamps and the new front indicator and sidelight units. But the future for this independent coachbuilder was already looking bleak, and it bodied only 18 of the S3 Continental chassis. Just one other special body was built: a drop-head by the Swiss firm of Graber that was not delivered until 1967.

MODELS: Fixed-head coupé, drophead coupé, Flying Spur, chassis for coachbuilders.
ENGINE: 6230cc OHV V8, twin SU carburettors, 215-235bhp (estimated).
GEARBOX: Four-speed GM Hydramatic automatic with fluid coupling.
SUSPENSION, STEERING & BRAKES: Independent front suspension with coil springs, wishbones and anti-roll bar, rear suspension with semi-elliptic leaf springs on 'live' axle, hydraulic dampers all round, with manual control at the rear. Cam-and-roller steering with hydraulic power assistance. Drum brakes front and rear, hydraulic at the front and hydro-mechanical at the rear, mechanical servo.
DIMENSIONS: Length: 17ft 8in (5385mm). **Width:** 6ft 2¾in (1898mm). **Height:** dependent on bodywork fitted. **Wheelbase:** 10ft 3in (3124mm). **Track:** front, 4ft 10½in (1486mm), rear, 5ft 0in (1524mm).
PERFORMANCE & FUEL CONSUMPTION: 117mph, 0-60mph in 10.8 sec, 12-13mpg.
PRODUCTION TOTAL: 311.

T SERIES

Rolls-Royce and Bentley design took a major leap forward with the Silver Shadow and T Series twins in late 1965, which had been developed with the internal code of SY. However, the arrival of these new models also signified a low point for the Bentley marque. Bentley derivatives had been pushed into the background during the S3 era, and the new T Series (not T Type) was to be no more than a slightly cheaper version of its Rolls-Royce sibling, a sop to Bentley traditionalists.

The differences between the two cars were reduced to their radiator grilles, bonnets to suit (the Bentley's was more curved) and badges. Sales reflected the manufacturer's lack of interest in the Bentley marque: in 1965, around 40 per cent of Crewe's production had worn Bentley badges, but that figure dropped to around 8 per cent over the life of the T Series.

The key innovation of the two new models was their dependence on a monocoque bodyshell instead of traditional separate chassis and body construction. The change kept Crewe abreast of the latest developments, but it was also hugely expensive. This high cost ensured there would be no separate Continental model, although the shared four-door design would later be supplemented by two-door saloon and drop-head coupé derivatives.

The T Series cars were much less curvaceous than the models they replaced, but still looked suitably impressive.

Engine and suspension were mounted on subframes beneath the monocoque bodyshell, which was built by Pressed Steel from steel and alloy. The styling, by John Blatchley at Crewe, lacked the curves of the previous range but remained discreet and imposing, while the cars offered both more passenger space and more boot space within more compact overall dimensions.

The V8 engine and automatic gearbox were carried over from the previous models, although engine power was increased slightly and LHD cars had a three-speed GM TurboHydramatic gearbox with torque

US models required side marker lights, and these were later standardised for all models (though without the bulb units outside the US). This is a 1973 car. (Calreyn88, CCA-SA 4.0)

converter instead of the fluid-flywheel four-speed. All-round independent suspension with a hydraulic self-levelling system that depended on Citroën patents was new. The same engine-driven high-pressure hydraulic system also powered the braking system, with discs on all four wheels for the first time.

For most countries, the radiator grille was still surmounted by a winged-B mascot. The T Series was the last model to which it was fitted.

T Series, 1965-1977

The Bentley T Series was announced alongside its Rolls-Royce sibling at the Paris Motor Show in early October 1965, although customer deliveries did not begin before spring 1966. Production lasted ten years until the cars were replaced by further developed T2 models, but there was a constant process of revision. The two factors that drove the major changes were customer demand for better handling dynamics and the changing safety and exhaust emissions requirements of the US market.

During 1968, the three-speed automatic was made standard for all cars. From May 1969, the US Federal specification was also standardised to reduce costs and assembly-line complication. From 1970, the enlarged 6750cc V8 engine pioneered in the Corniche became standard, to counter the effect of emissions control equipment. A revised 'compliant' suspension from mid-1972 allowed the use of radial tyres without increasing noise levels, and further revisions in spring 1974 brought lower-profile tyres with wider tracks and slightly flared wheelarch lips to accommodate them. From mid-1973, cars destined for the US also took on large black impact bumpers, which met a federal requirement that bumpers should protect the bodywork and lights from damage in a low-speed impact. These bumpers were mounted on damper struts that controlled the force with which they could be pushed in towards the body.

Meanwhile, a long-wheelbase model, created by literally cutting a standard monocoque in half and inserting four extra inches, became available from May 1969. Like

A sumptuous interior was expected, and the T Series delivered. Only details distinguished it from the Rolls-Royce equivalent. (Anchornetwork CCA-SA 3.0)

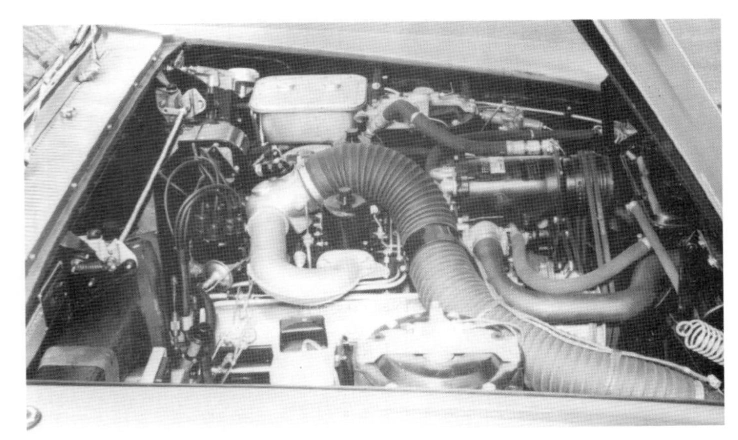

Under the bonnet was the latest version of the 6230cc V8 engine, its rocker covers branded with the Bentley name. A 6750cc version replaced it in 1970.

their Rolls-Royce equivalents, these cars had a smaller rear window and an Everflex vinyl roof covering, and could be ordered with or without a division. Few were made: customers preferred their limousines with Rolls-Royce badges.

The monocoque construction of the T Series made bespoke coachwork impractical: none of the independent coachbuilders could afford to develop the special monocoque bodies that would have been required. Nevertheless, Crewe did supply a number of complete saloons in the early days for James Young to convert into two-door types, and Pininfarina built a single special body on a T Series. As noted above, Crewe abandoned the idea of creating a special Continental variant, and settled instead for special two-door bodies built by its Mulliner, Park Ward division. All these special variants are discussed separately below.

The last of the original T Series Bentleys were built in early 1977, and from February the revised T2 models took over.

MODELS: Four-door saloon, long-wheelbase saloon.
ENGINE: 6230cc V8 (1965-1970), twin SU carburettors, 205-210bhp (estimated), 6750cc V8 (1970-1977), twin SU carburettors, 210-220bhp (estimated).
TRANSMISSION: Four-speed automatic gearbox (RHD to summer 1968), three-speed automatic gearbox (all LHD, and RHD from summer 1968). Rear-wheel drive.
SUSPENSION, STEERING & BRAKES: Front suspension with coil springs, wishbones and anti-roll bar. Rear suspension with coil springs and semi-trailing arms, anti-roll bar from 1968. Hydraulic self-levelling front and rear, rear only from summer 1969. Recirculating ball steering with hydraulic power assistance. Disc brakes front and rear, with high-pressure hydraulic power assistance.
DIMENSIONS: Length: standard cars, 16ft 11.5in (5169mm), long-wheelbase, 17ft 3.5in (5370mm). **Width:** 5ft 11in (1803mm) to spring 1974, 5ft 11.7in (1821mm) from spring 1974. **Height:** 4ft 11.75in (1518mm). **Wheelbase:** 9ft 11.5in (3035mm); standard cars, 10ft 0in (3048mm) from spring 1974; 10ft 3.5in (3137mm); long-wheelbase, 10ft 4in (3150mm) from spring 1974. **Track:** front and rear, 4ft 9.5in (1460mm).
PERFORMANCE & FUEL CONSUMPTION: 115mph, 0-60mph in 10.9 sec, 15mpg.
PRODUCTION TOTALS: 1703 (standard saloon), 9 (long-wheelbase saloon).

James Young T Series, 1966-1967

The decision to switch to monocoque construction dealt the death blow to Britain's remaining coachbuilders. Traditional coachbuilding depended on a separate chassis, and the cost of constructing a monocoque body to individual specifications made the whole exercise impractical.

James Young's brave two-door conversion retained the overall lines of the parent saloon.

Hooper's closure in 1959 was largely driven by the news that the mainstream Rolls-Royce and Bentley models would in future have monocoque construction, and that year H J Mulliner sold out to Rolls-Royce to safeguard its future. Two years later, it would be merged with the other coachbuilder the company owned to become the Mulliner, Park Ward division.

Of the major British coachbuilders, that left just James Young, which struggled on by supplying coachwork for the Rolls-Royce Phantom V and Phantom VI limousine chassis. The company matched this bravery with a two-door conversion of the T Series and its Rolls-Royce equivalent, which it introduced in 1966, just before the in-house two-door model went on sale.

The James Young T Series was a straightforward conversion of the standard four-door saloon, with a single long door on each side in place of the two doors of the factory-produced car. There were modifications inside, such as tipping front seats to afford access to the rear, but otherwise the cars were unchanged. There was no question about their exclusivity, but they looked too similar to the standard saloon to have any appeal beyond that. Just 15 Bentley T Series conversions were built (plus 35 Rolls-Royce types) before James Young closed down for good in 1968.

MODEL: Two-door saloon.
ENGINE: 6230cc V8, twin SU carburettors, 205-210bhp (estimated).
GEARBOX: Four-speed Hydramatic (RHD), three-speed GM400 automatic (LHD).
SUSPENSION, STEERING & BRAKES: Front suspension with coil springs, wishbones and anti-roll bar. Rear suspension with coil springs and semi-trailing arms. Recirculating ball steering with hydraulic power assistance. Disc brakes front and rear, with high-pressure hydraulic power assistance.
DIMENSIONS: Length: 16ft 11½in (5169mm). **Width:** 5ft 11in (1803mm). **Height:** 4ft 11¾in (1518mm). **Wheelbase:** 9ft 11½in (3035mm). **Track:** front and rear, 4ft 9.5in (1460mm).
PERFORMANCE & FUEL CONSUMPTION: 115mph, 0-60mph in 10.9 sec, 15mpg.
PRODUCTION TOTAL: 15.

Mulliner Park Ward T Series, 1966-1971

Even though a separate Bentley Continental variant of the T Series had been ruled out, Rolls-Royce knew there would be demand for a two-door derivative of the new car. John Blatchley's styling department at Crewe therefore drew up a two-door style that would be suitable for both open and closed bodies, and would be made with both Bentley and Rolls-Royce badges. The front end styling was deliberately similar to that of the Silver Shadow and T Series, but a new and curvaceous side profile with a more rounded

Subtle wing styling lines gave the Mulliner, Park Ward models their individual look. The convertible roof was a particularly neat creation. (Anton van Luijk, CCA 2.0)

tail gave the two-door bodies a very different character.

The job of building these cars was entrusted to the Mulliner, Park Ward coachbuilding division, which completely reorganised its factory to construct the all-welded, all-steel bodies in jigs and mount them on platforms provided by Pressed Steel. Despite the new production methods in use, these cars were still very much hand-made creations with individual craftsman features, and each took about 20 weeks to build.

The closed version of the new model was introduced first, in March 1966, and was known as a Bentley T Series Mulliner Park Ward Two-door Saloon. In the US, it was often described more succinctly as a coupé. The drop-head coupé followed over a year later in September 1967. Both could be ordered in either Bentley or Rolls-Royce guise, and in each case the Bentley was slightly less expensive than the Rolls-Royce derivative, which nevertheless sold much more strongly.

The drop-head coupé had identical body lines to the two-door saloon, but its underside and sills were heavily strengthened to compensate for the absence of a fixed roof. Its elegant hood came with power operation as standard.

Specification changes during production paralleled those for the T Series four-door saloons, but as a matter of policy appeared slightly earlier on the two-door cars. An exception was that the two-door saloons gained a rear anti-roll bar in 1968, but the drop-heads did not get one until mid-1970.

Production of these models in their original guise ended in 1971, but they were then continued, with several improvements, as Bentley Corniche types.

MODELS: Two-door saloon (coupé), drop-head coupé.
ENGINE: 6230cc V8, twin SU carburettors, 200-220bhp (estimated).
GEARBOX: Four-speed Hydramatic (RHD to summer 1968), three-speed GM400 automatic (all LHD, and RHD from summer 1968).
SUSPENSION, STEERING & BRAKES: Front suspension with coil springs, wishbones and anti-roll bar. Rear suspension with coil springs

The interior of the drop-head coupé was once again outfitted with every luxury of the day.

In open form, the drop-head coupé had a prestigious look of its own. This is an early US car, with the early style of side markers.

and semi-trailing arms, anti-roll bar from 1968. Hydraulic self-levelling front and rear, rear only from summer 1969. Recirculating ball steering with hydraulic power assistance. Disc brakes front and rear, with high-pressure hydraulic power assistance.
DIMENSIONS: Length: 16ft 11.5in (5169mm). **Width:** 5ft 11in (1803mm). **Height:** saloon, 4ft 10.75in (1492mm), drop-head coupé, 4ft 11.75in (1518mm). **Wheelbase:** 9ft 11.5in (3035mm). **Track:** front and rear, 4ft 9.5in (1460mm).
PERFORMANCE & FUEL CONSUMPTION: 115mph, 0-60mph in 10.9 sec, 15mpg.
PRODUCTION TOTALS: 98 (saloon), 41 (drop-head coupé).

Pininfarina T Series, 1968

Not all the major coachbuilders had thrown in the towel as the motor industry had gone over to monocoque bodies, and one company that had adapted to the new conditions was the Italian coachbuilder Pininfarina. To showcase its talents, this company ordered a RHD T Series four-door underframe in late 1967 or early 1968, with the intention of turning it into a show special.

The car was completed as a two-door coupé with sloping rear roofline, and was displayed at the 1968 Turin Motor Show as a 'coupé Speciale'. It was subsequently bought by the industrialist James Hanson (later Lord Hanson). After onward sale through H R Owen in London during 1980, it was fitted with black bumpers as used on the later T2 models and with Corniche-stye wheel trims. Some commentators have suggested that this car inspired Pininfarina's design for the Rolls-Royce Camargue.

Mechanical specifications as for standard T Series. Dimensions and performance figures not available.
PRODUCTION TOTAL: 1 only.

Pininfarina built just one show special on the T Series platform – the fastback coupé seen here. (Stephen Foskett/Wikimedia)

Corniche, 1971-1984

The two-door saloons and drop-head coupés that Mulliner, Park Ward built on the T Series platform satisfied demand for a time, but they lacked the strong identity of their Continental predecessors. Crewe decided to give them a clearer identity of their own by giving them the name of Corniche, which had been planned over 30 years earlier for the car that anticipated the Continental.

This was still a time when the Bentley marque was seen as a less prestigious alternative to Rolls-Royce, and the Corniche was therefore put on sale with both marque identities – the first time a Bentley and a Rolls-Royce had shared a model name. At the media launch in March 1971, the Rolls-Royce version was highlighted, with the result that few people realised a Bentley version was actually available. The Corniche as a model was a huge success: waiting lists soon formed and early cars were resold for up 80 per cent on top of their original cost price. However, the Bentley Corniche would always be very much rarer than its Rolls-Royce counterpart.

Central to the Corniche was a new 6750cc version of the V8 engine, which was tuned to give around 10 per cent more power than its saloon equivalent. Changes to valve and ignition timing, a less restrictive air silencer and a larger-bore exhaust system made the differences, but US emissions regulations ensured the higher-power engines were denied to US customers.

The wheel trims help to identify this two-door saloon as an early Corniche. (Jeremy, CCA 2.0)

The bodyshells of both two-door saloon and drop-head coupé were carried over from the earlier cars, but a series of minor revisions made them appear quite distinctive. Most obvious were the new wheel trims made from spun stainless steel, with a design that aided brake cooling. There was a discreet Corniche plate badge on the tail, and an extra half inch in the depth of the radiator shell, and the saloon variants could be had optionally with

This 1974 Corniche drop-head is a US model, with side marker lights and 'impact' bumpers. (Mr.choppers/CCA-SA 3.0)

Again a US model, this Corniche saloon displays the two-tone colour split that was an option.

an Everflex roof covering that added further distinction and was a fashionable feature at the time.

On the inside, there was also a new dashboard, which came with a rev counter on both Bentley and Rolls-Royce variants, although this was soon deleted. There was a three-spoke steering wheel with wood rim but that was also deleted in August 1971, when it gave way to a 16in wheel with a black plastic rim.

Thereafter, the usual process of gradual improvements began. From 1972, ventilated front disc brakes became standard. For the 1974 model-year, US cars gained black impact bumpers and a shorter radiator shell to allow the bumper blade to move, and the air intakes below the headlamps were deleted. The 1975 models for most markets had a new Solex carburettor and breakerless ignition and the 1976 cars had the same engine changes as the saloons.

For 1976, the Corniche took on a new facia and split-level air-conditioning and, in spring 1977, rack-and-pinion steering became standard, as did the large black bumpers. A major change came in March 1979, when the rear suspension and subframe were modified to the latest SZ (Bentley Mulsanne) type and the hydraulic systems switched from conventional brake fluid to mineral oil. Saloon models went out of production at the end of 1980, but the drop-head coupés remained available. The US and some other countries had Bosch injection instead of carburettors for 1981, and thus revised the range continued until 1984, when the Bentley drop-head models were continued under the Continental name.

It is interesting that Crewe seriously considered updating the Corniche by giving it a front end similar to that of the latest SZ models, but the full-size mock-up proved disappointing. The original design was therefore retained.

MODELS: Two-door saloon (coupé), drop-head coupé.
ENGINE: 6750cc V8 with 240bhp (estimated), injected engines with 237bhp. Two SU carburettors, or (from 1980 for US-specification cars) Bosch K-Jetronic fuel injection.
GEARBOX: Three-speed GM400 automatic .
SUSPENSION, STEERING & BRAKES: Front suspension with coil springs, wishbones and anti-roll bar. Rear suspension with coil springs, semi-trailing arms, and high-pressure hydraulic self-levelling system. Power-assisted rack-and-pinion steering. Disc brakes front and rear, with high-pressure hydraulic power assistance.
DIMENSIONS: Length: 16ft 11.5in (5169mm) to March 1977, 17ft 0.5in (5194mm) from March 1977. **Width:** 5ft 11.7in (1821mm). **Height:** 4ft 11.75in (1518mm). **Wheelbase:** 9ft 11.75in (3042mm) to 1974, 10ft 0in (3048mm) from 1974 to 1979, 10ft 0.5in (3061mm) from 1979. **Track:** front, 5ft 0in (1524mm), rear, 4ft 11.6in (1514mm).
PERFORMANCE & FUEL CONSUMPTION: 119mph, 0-60mph in 10.1 sec, 14.5mpg.
PRODUCTION TOTALS: 63 (saloon), 77 (drop-head coupé).

T2, 1977-1980

For the last three years of its production, the T Series was revised with a number of improvements and changes that collectively earned the model the new name of T2. Introduced in early 1977, this final version of the range came with a new power-assisted rack-and-pinion steering system, plus revised front suspension geometry and a smaller-diameter rear anti-roll bar to deliver much sharper steering.

Streamlining production again, the factory

The black bumpers and front air dam help to identify this as a Bentley T2 model. Note, too, the headlamp wash-wipe system.

This US-specification T2 saloon shows the 'Bentley T2' badge on the boot lid, and the special US number-plate holder. (Stanzilla, CCA-SA 3.0)

now fitted large black impact bumpers as standard for all markets – although only those for the US were mounted on the damper struts that had been used since their introduction on the 1974-model T Series cars for the US. From 1978, a headlamp wash-wipe system became standard, in this case using items that had been available on cars for Scandinavian countries for some years.

A major change to the interior added the split-level air-conditioning system introduced earlier on the Corniche models, and with this came a new facia. It incorporated a distinctive panel of warning lights alongside the traditional twin dial instruments and, to meet US safety regulations, was no longer made of solid wood but of wood veneer on an alloy armature.

For most countries, the T2 retained its twin SU carburettors to the end, but from late 1979 the last cars for California had a Bosch CIS fuel injection system, which was the only way of meeting that state's uniquely tight emissions regulations. Cars for other US states followed suit for 1981.

Sales of the Bentley T2 remained very much lower than those of the Rolls-Royce equivalent, although there was a surprise increase in the number of orders for the long-

Two-tone paintwork remained available for the T2, and is seen on this 1978 example.

wheelbase versions. Ten of these were made, still with the same four extra inches in the wheelbase, Everflex vinyl roof, and smaller rear window to afford the rear-seat occupants extra privacy.

MODELS: Four-door saloon, long-wheelbase saloon.
ENGINE: 6750cc V8 with 240bhp (estimated). Two SU carburettors, or (from 1980 for US-specification cars) Bosch K-Jetronic fuel injection.
GEARBOX: Three-speed GM400 automatic.
SUSPENSION, STEERING & BRAKES: Front suspension with coil springs, wishbones and anti-roll bar. Rear suspension with coil springs, semi-trailing arms, and high-pressure hydraulic self-levelling system. Power-assisted rack-and-pinion steering. Disc brakes front and rear, with high-pressure hydraulic power assistance.
DIMENSIONS: Length: standard cars, 17ft 0.5in (5194mm), long-wheelbase, 17ft 4.5in (5296mm). **Width:** 5ft 11.7in (1821mm). **Height:** 4ft 11.75in (1518mm). **Wheelbase:** standard cars, 10ft 0in (3050mm), long-wheelbase, 10ft 4in (3150mm). **Track:** front, 5ft 0in (1524mm), rear, 59.6in (1514mm).
PERFORMANCE & FUEL CONSUMPTION: 119mph, 0-60mph in 10.1 sec, 14.5mpg.
PRODUCTION TOTALS: 558 (standard saloon), 10 (long-wheelbase).

Continental, 1984-1994

By the early 1980s, Crewe had embarked on its plan to revive the Bentley marque and to make its models more different from those with Rolls-Royce badges. As an early stage in this process, the Bentley versions of the Corniche (by then sold only in drop-head form) were renamed Bentley Continental in summer 1984, reviving the name last used nearly 20 years earlier for the more sporting variants of the Bentley chassis.

Their subsequent development largely paralleled that of the Rolls-Royce equivalent, which retained the Corniche name, and production continued for ten more years. Of interest is that some consideration was given in 1986 to a derivative with a GRP hardtop fixed in place, in effect reviving the Corniche saloon that had gone out of production in 1980. The idea was not approved for production.

With the new Continental name came some visual changes, as grille slats, bumpers and mirror bodies were all painted in the body colour, and slim, bright metal trims were also added to the wheelarch edges. There were also further revisions to the seats and dashboard. For the 1986 season, striking new alloy wheels became standard and, for 1987, fuel injection became universal. The 1987 engines gave 22 per cent more power than the earlier carburettor types, and all 1987 models except those for North America had ABS as standard.

There were more interior revisions on the 1987 models, and further interior changes for the 1989 cars accompanied a stiffened

Subtly modified, with alloy wheels, a front air dam, and bright wheelarch trims, this is the later Bentley Continental drop-head coupé.

Pictured in all its splendour, this 1985 Continental once belonged to singer Elton John, whose name is referred to in its number plate.

cylinder block and an uprated gearbox. For 1990, the engine management system changed to a Bosch Motronic type, and for 1992 the Continental models gained the automatic ride control system that had been available on saloons since October 1989. The 1992 cars took on a new GM 4L80E four-speed gearbox with electronic control, and the last cars were built in 1994.

MODEL: Drop-head coupé.
ENGINE: 6750cc V8 with 240bhp (estimated), 290bhp (estimated) from 1987. Solex 4A1 carburettor, or (for all US-specification cars and standard from 1987) Bosch K-Jetronic fuel injection.
GEARBOX: Three-speed GM400 automatic (1984-1992), four-speed GM GL480-E automatic (1992-1994).
SUSPENSION, STEERING & BRAKES: Front suspension with coil springs, wishbones and anti-roll bar. Rear suspension with coil springs, semi-trailing arms, and high-pressure hydraulic self-levelling system. Power-assisted rack-and-pinion steering. Disc brakes front and rear, with high-pressure hydraulic power assistance.
DIMENSIONS: Length: 17ft 0.5in (5194mm). **Width:** 6ft 0in (1829mm). **Height:** 4ft 11.75in (1518mm). **Wheelbase:** 10ft 0in (3050mm). **Track:** front, 5ft 0in (1524mm), rear, 4ft 11.6in (1514mm).

Rear head restraints were added to later Continentals, like this 1988 model pictured in the Netherlands. (AlfvanBeem/Public Domain)

This rear view of a 1988 Continental in the US shows how later models for that country had a rather inelegant third brake light positioned on the boot lid. (Mr.choppers/CCA-SA 3.0)

PERFORMANCE & FUEL CONSUMPTION: 120mph, 0-60mph in 9.6 sec, 14mpg.
PRODUCTION TOTAL: 421.

Camargue, 1985

The Bentley Camargue was never a catalogued model, but a single car was built in 1985 to special order for the Sultan of Brunei, for whom Crewe would later go on to undertake a large number of individual commissions.

The Camargue was only ever catalogued as a Rolls-Royce, and from its origins was intended as a flagship coupé that would embody the very latest technology and appeal to a small number of customers determined to have not only the best but also a car that was very distinctive. It was based on the underframe and running gear of the SY (Silver Shadow and T Series) family, and its body design was done by the Italian styling house of Pininfarina.

Interestingly, all the Camargue prototypes were disguised with Bentley-style grilles when they were out on test, because this supposedly made them less conspicuous. A total of 530 production cars left Crewe between 1975 and 1985, and the special-order Bentley was one of the last to be built.

The Bentley grille certainly suited the proportions of the Pininfarina body very well, and probably rather better than the Rolls-Royce grille did. In later years, as Camargue prices fell, several owners had their cars fitted with Bentley grilles and other markings in an attempt to make them more distinctive.

MODEL: Two-door coupé.
ENGINE: 6750cc V8 with 237bhp, Solex 4A1 carburettor.
GEARBOX: Three-speed GM400 automatic.
SUSPENSION, STEERING & BRAKES: Front suspension with coil springs, wishbones and anti-roll bar. Rear suspension with coil springs, semi-trailing arms, and high-pressure hydraulic self-levelling system. Power-assisted rack-and-pinion steering. Disc brakes front and rear, with high-pressure hydraulic power assistance.
DIMENSIONS: Length: 17ft 0.5in (5194mm). **Width:** 6ft 3.5in (1918mm). **Height:** 4ft 10in (1473mm). **Wheelbase:** 10ft 0.5in (3061mm). **Track:** front, 5ft 0in (1524mm), rear, 4ft 11.6in (1514mm).
PERFORMANCE & FUEL CONSUMPTION: 119mph, 0-60mph in 10.1 sec, 14.5mpg.
PRODUCTION TOTAL: 1 only.

Continental Turbo, 1992-1995

The Continental Turbo was not initially intended as a catalogued model, and started life as a batch of three cars built to special order for the Sultan of Brunei between 1992 and 1995. However, five more cars were later built for public sale, and the basic specification was also used for the limited-edition Rolls-Royce Corniche S introduced in summer 1995 with the turbocharged engine to mark the end of Corniche production.

The turbocharged engine fitted to these cars was the latest 328bhp variant of the 6750cc V8, and it was given an exhaust system based on that of the contemporary Turbo R. The three cars built for the Sultan also had stiffened body sills to cope with additional torsional stresses, and were fitted with the 16in wheels and low-profile tyres of the Continental R. Probably all eight cars had the automatic ride control system that was introduced on other models in 1992.

MODEL: Drophead coupé.
ENGINE: 6750cc V8 with 328bhp, Bosch MK-Motronic fuel injection.
GEARBOX: Four-speed GM GL480-E automatic.
SUSPENSION, STEERING & BRAKES: Front suspension with coil springs, wishbones and anti-roll bar. Rear suspension with coil springs, semi-trailing arms, and high-pressure hydraulic self-levelling system. Power-assisted rack-and-pinion steering. Disc brakes front and rear, with high-pressure hydraulic power assistance.
DIMENSIONS: Length: 17ft 0.5in (5194mm). **Width:** 6ft 0in/72in (1829mm). **Height:** 4ft 11.75in (1518mm). **Wheelbase:** 10ft 0in (3050mm). **Track:** front, 5ft 0in (1524mm), rear, 59.6in (1514mm).
PERFORMANCE & FUEL CONSUMPTION: No figures available.
PRODUCTION TOTAL: 8.

THE MULSANNE (SZ) FAMILY

When work began on the next generation of saloons from Crewe in 1969, the Bentley marque was still considered the poor relation and, in fact, no Bentley version of the new model was even considered until quite late in the design process.

There were cost constraints on the new design, which Crewe knew as the SZ type, and so large elements of the SY (Silver Shadow and T Series) cars had to be carried over. The underframe, suspension and powertrain could have only evolutionary changes, but notable among them were the redesigned rear suspension and subframe.

The appearance was radically changed, though, under the direction of Fritz Feller, who had taken over from John Blatchley. An aim was to make the SZ look lower and more rounded than the SY range, to give it greater presence. Ironically, most of the eight prototypes had dummy Bentley grilles, as was then the practice at Crewe.

The only hint of what might come later was the decision to give the car a name of its own instead of a letter type. That name was Mulsanne, after the famous straight section of the Le Mans racing circuit where Bentley had made its name in competition in the 1920s.

Mulsanne, 1980-1987

As announced in October 1980, the Mulsanne was a direct clone of the new Rolls-Royce Silver Spirit, the only obvious differences lying in the grille and badges. Less obvious was that the front bumper had slightly more curvature to provide effective protection for the Bentley grille. Sadly, the winged B mascot was now absent, banished by safety legislation.

The Mulsanne itself was never sold in the US, although later Bentley members of the SZ range were – and its use of an American-style foot-operated parking brake in place of the traditional twist-grip handbrake might have alerted commentators that greater things were planned. Production changes for the first few years were limited after the arrival of a Refinement Package in 1981, as the factory focused on the new Mulsanne Turbo, the

The original Mulsanne, introduced in October 1980, looked quite tame by later standards.

Eight and the Mulsanne Turbo R derivatives. June 1981 also brought the inevitable long-wheelbase models, with an extra four inches in the wheelbase that improved rear legroom. These bodyshells were not converted as those for the SY range had been, but were specially built by Pressed Steel at Cowley.

For the 1986 season, the Mulsanne took on the new suspension that had been developed for the Bentley Turbo R, which very much improved the handling. The front number plate moved to the centre of the bumper and headlamp washers replaced the original wash-wipe system. The 1987 models gained that season's improvements, although production delays meant that relatively few were built with the final specification. This included K-Jetronic fuel injection that boosted power to 238bhp, taller axle gearing, ABS and the wider wheels and tyres of the Turbo R.

The replacement model for the original Mulsanne was the Mulsanne S.

MODELS: Four-door saloon, long-wheelbase saloon.
ENGINE: 6750cc V8 with 198bhp (estimated, 1980-1986) or 238bhp (estimated, 1987). Two SU carburettors (1980-1986), 1987 models with Bosch K-Jetronic fuel injection.
GEARBOX: Three-speed GM400 automatic.
SUSPENSION, STEERING & BRAKES: Front suspension with coil springs, wishbones and anti-roll bar. Rear suspension with coil springs, semi-trailing arms, anti-roll bar, and high-pressure hydraulic self-levelling system. Power-assisted rack-and-pinion steering. Ventilated front disc brakes and solid rear disc brakes, with high-pressure hydraulic power assistance. Bosch ABS from 1986.

DIMENSIONS: Length: standard cars, 17ft 5in (5309mm); long-wheelbase, 17ft 9in (5411mm). **Width:** 6ft 2.3in (1887mm) over body, 6ft 7in (2008mm) over door mirrors. **Height:** 4ft 10.75in (1492mm). **Wheelbase:** standard cars, 10ft 0.5in (3061mm); long-wheelbase, 10ft 4.5in (3162mm). **Track:** 5ft 0.5in (1537mm).
PERFORMANCE & FUEL CONSUMPTION: 115mph, 0-60mph in 10.3 sec, 14-16mpg.
PRODUCTION TOTALS: 482 (standard saloon); 49 (long-wheelbase).

The body-colour grille surround marks this 1982 car out as a Mulsanne Turbo.

Mulsanne Turbo, 1982-1985

The Mulsanne Turbo introduced in 1982 had a fundamental role in reviving the Bentley marque. Though far from flawless, it added a completely new level of straight-line performance to the existing Mulsanne, and made clear what direction future Bentley models would take. Importantly, it had no Rolls-Royce counterpart.

Turbocharging the existing V8 engine was an obvious and cost-effective solution to gaining extra performance, and a first turbocharged prototype was built in 1977. Development was done with the aid of Broadspeed before being taken back in-house for final refinements. With a Solex four-barrel carburettor, a single Garrett turbocharger – there was insufficient space for two – and a large-diameter twin exhaust system, the engine delivered 298bhp, and was governed to give the Mulsanne Turbo a 135mph top speed. Long-wheelbase versions may have been slightly slower – but not many people bought one to find out.

To match this power and performance, the three-speed gearbox had a strengthened torque converter and uprated rear axle components, and the car ran on specially-designed Avon Turbospeed tyres. A tall final drive made for more restful cruising, but did not inhibit the 0-100mph acceleration of 18 seconds. The only major disappointment was the handling – but improvements were in the pipeline. As for appearance, the Mulsanne Turbo was as discreet as customers expected, its only special features being a body-coloured surround to the radiator grille and a 'Turbo' plate badge on the boot lid.

From July 1984, the suspension was stiffened, but this was only a step in the right direction. Further changes in preparation

The presence of the turbocharged engine was clearly indicated under the bonnet.

This later Mulsanne Turbo has alloy wheels. The discreet Turbo plate badge is visible on the right of the boot lid.

would deliver the Turbo R model, which replaced the original Mulsanne Turbo in October 1985. In the meantime, the Mulsanne Turbo did exactly what it was supposed to do. Together with the new Bentley Continental introduced in 1984, it raised the proportion of Bentley models built at Crewe to 22 per cent by late 1985 – a huge improvement over the 5 per cent figure posted around the time of the Turbo's introduction in 1982.

MODELS: Four-door saloon, long-wheelbase saloon.
ENGINE: 6750cc V8 with 298bhp. Solex four-barrel carburettor and single Garrett turbocharger.
GEARBOX: Three-speed GM400 automatic.
SUSPENSION, STEERING & BRAKES: Front suspension with coil springs, wishbones and anti-roll bar. Rear suspension with coil springs, semi-trailing arms, anti-roll bar, and high-pressure hydraulic self-levelling system. Power-assisted rack-and-pinion steering. Ventilated front disc brakes and solid rear disc brakes, with high-pressure hydraulic power assistance. Bosch ABS from 1986.
DIMENSIONS: Length: standard cars, 17ft 5in (5309mm), long-wheelbase, 17ft 9in (5411mm). **Width:** 6ft 2.3in (1887mm) over body, 6ft 7in (2008mm) over door mirrors. **Height:** 4ft 10.75in (1492mm). **Wheelbase:** standard cars, 10 ft 0.5in (3061mm), long-wheelbase, 10ft 4.5in (3162mm). **Track:** 5ft 0.5in (1537mm).
PERFORMANCE & FUEL CONSUMPTION: 135mph, 0-60mph in 7.0 sec, 12-15mpg.
PRODUCTION TOTALS: 495 (standard saloon), 24 (long-wheelbase).

Eight, 1984-1992

Introduced in July 1984, the Bentley Eight was another step in the revival of the Bentley marque. It was essentially an entry-level derivative of the Mulsanne that had been carefully prepared to make the car more appealing to a new type of customer; with the Eight, Bentley aimed to attract younger buyers away from BMW and Mercedes luxury saloons. The new model was available only to British buyers for the first nine months, and there were no export models before March 1985. From November 1986, it was used to spearhead Bentley's reintroduction to the US market.

Although this was no cut-price luxury car, its cost was kept down by subtle deletions: among other things, there were steel instead of alloy wheels, the wood trim was less expensive, the dashboard was simpler, and the standard upholstery was cloth rather than leather. On the positive side, however, the car

The Eight brought down the entry price for a Mulsanne derivative in 1984. The mesh grille was a distinguishing feature.

The Mulsanne dash, even on the entry-level Eight as shown here, featured the expected polished wood.

started life with the revised suspension also introduced for the Mulsanne Turbo in summer 1984, giving it the tauter handling that Crewe believed would appeal to its target audience.

The Bentley Eight was readily recognisable by a chrome mesh grille in place of the standard slatted type, a styling device designed to remind onlookers of the mesh grilles used on the later Le Mans racing Bentleys of the 1920s. The car also had a plate badge on the boot lid that read 'Eight'.

From October 1985, the suspension was stiffened to match that of the Turbo R, and the revised cars were recognisable by the repositioned front number plate, which moved to the centre of the bumper from its earlier position underneath. The 1987 model-year Eight took on fuel injection and taller gearing, and the 1988 and later models came with leather upholstery as standard. From 1989, the cars had alloy wheels and twinned rectangular headlamp units; 1990 brought the automatic ride height system and the option of catalytic converters. Eights took on the new four-speed 4L-80E gearbox in August 1992, together with a high-level third brake light. Production ended in January 1993.

MODELS: Four-door saloon.
ENGINE: 6750cc V8 with 198bhp (estimated, 1984-1986) or 205bhp (estimated, from 1987). Two SU carburettors (1984-1986); 1987 and later models with Bosch K-Jetronic fuel injection.
GEARBOX: Three-speed GM400 automatic. Four-speed GM 4L80-E automatic from 1992.
SUSPENSION, STEERING & BRAKES: Front

This 1989-model Eight shows the new paired headlamps and alloy wheels.

suspension with coil springs, wishbones and anti-roll bar. Rear suspension with coil springs, semi-trailing arms, anti-roll bar, and high-pressure hydraulic self-levelling system. Power-assisted rack-and-pinion steering. Ventilated front disc brakes and solid rear disc brakes, with high-pressure hydraulic power assistance. Bosch ABS from 1986.
DIMENSIONS: Length: 17ft 5in (5309mm). **Width:** 6ft 2.3in (1887mm) over body, 6ft 7in (2008mm) over door mirrors. **Height:** 4ft 10.75in (1492mm). **Wheelbase:** 10 ft 0.5in (3061mm). **Track:** 5ft 0.5in (1537mm).
PERFORMANCE & FUEL CONSUMPTION: 126mph, 0-60mph in 11 sec, 12-14mpg.
PRODUCTION TOTAL: 1736.

Turbo R, 1985-1997

The Turbo R was the second-stage evolution of the Mulsanne Turbo, incorporating changes suggested by customer feedback on the earlier cars. The most important of these was a revised suspension that gave rise to the R designation: the letter supposedly and deservedly stood for Roadholding, which in this new model was vastly improved over that of the standard SZ models. The Turbo R immediately became the most expensive Bentley variant of the SZ range, and the standard car was accompanied by a long-wheelbase variant, which was nevertheless little known beyond its own customer base.

The Turbo R was previewed at the Geneva Show in March 1985 and went on sale in October. Its tauter suspension consisted of new anti-roll bars and firmer dampers, plus a Panhard rod at the rear and hydraulic damping between the tops of the self-levelling struts. Steering feel was improved by a reduction of power assistance. These were also the first Bentley models to have alloy wheels, which had wider rims than their steel predecessors and were manufactured by Ronal in Germany. Specially-made tyres were part of the package, and a deeper front air dam helped the car to look the part. The cabin also had unique features – a special dashboard with a rev counter (recalling the Continentals of earlier times) and a full console between the front seats.

Further development of the Turbo R followed the same pattern as other members of the SZ family, although the Turbo R also had its own special features. When the standard SZ cars took on fuel injection for 1987, the Turbo R had its own specification with Bosch KE-Jetronic injection and twin distributors. Power increased by a further 10 per cent and was matched by a taller axle ratio; the 1987 models also came with a rev counter for the first time. The Turbo R was also released in the US in November 1988, where it joined the Eight and the Mulsanne S models, and in

The Turbo R was the first Bentley with alloy wheels, and retained the body-colour grille surround of the earlier Mulsanne Turbo.

The tail badge of the Turbo R did not reveal that it was the R model.

late 1991 or early 1992 the new four-speed automatic gearbox replaced the original three-speed type.

For 1989, a Bosch MK-Motronic engine management system and an air-to-air intercooler were added; maximum power increased by just over 10 per cent to 328bhp and there were important torque gains. The 1989 models also had twin round headlamps instead of rectangular ones. The 1990 season brought automatic ride control, and a catalytic converter became optional in July 1990.

For the first half of the 1990s, Turbo R development continued in small increments. The four-speed gearbox arrived in 1993 and, on the 1993 models, the automatic selector moved from the steering column to the centre console and 16in wheels with lower-profile tyres became standard. These cars were distinguished by green enamel badges. The 1994 cars reverted to red enamel badges and lost the bright bonnet centre strip, but also introduced important changes. These included Zytek fuel injection, redesigned seats and a passenger-side airbag as standard. Meanwhile, transient boost control gave a brief burst of some 20 per cent additional power for overtaking but protected the engine through a governed transition back to 'normal' mode. New adaptive shift control enabled the transmission control software to modify the shift points to suit the driver's style.

Changes for the 1996 model-year cars were more far-reaching, earning the name of 'new' Turbo R from Bentley. A redesigned bumper and air dam assembly with large mesh grilles accompanied a shortened radiator grille, and the spare wheel was moved into the boot, making way for a new rear bumper and valance assembly. The new bumpers and the side sills were all finished in body colour. As on other SZ models, the front doors lost their quarter-lights and gained more aerodynamic mirrors. There were also new 17in seven-spoke alloy wheels and multiple interior changes. The engine gained a Zytek management system, top speed was now limited to 150mph, and a viscous-coupled differential became standard.

The 1996 models included a limited-production Turbo R Sport for Germany on the standard wheelbase, with different alloy wheels (from the Continental T) and carbon fibre interior trim in place of the traditional wood. The 1997 model-year brought the last of the standard-wheelbase models, although the long-wheelbase Turbo R remained available into 1998 with an electronic traction control system and improved front brakes.

MODELS: Four-door saloon, long-wheelbase saloon.

ENGINE: 6750cc V8 with 328bhp. Solex four-barrel carburettor and single Garrett turbocharger. 1987 and later models with Bosch fuel injection. 1994 and later models with Zytek fuel injection.

GEARBOX: Three-speed

Although the gear selector was still on the column, the Turbo R had a sporty-looking centre console.

Looking the part: the 1997 Turbo R was the last one on the standard wheelbase.

GM400 automatic. Four-speed GM 4L80-E. automatic from 1992.
SUSPENSION, STEERING & BRAKES: Front suspension with coil springs, wishbones and anti-roll bar. Rear suspension with coil springs, semi-trailing arms, anti-roll bar, and high-pressure hydraulic self-levelling system. Power-assisted rack-and-pinion steering. Ventilated front disc brakes and solid rear disc brakes, with high-pressure hydraulic power assistance and Bosch ABS.
DIMENSIONS: Length: standard cars, 17ft 5in (5309mm), long-wheelbase, 17ft 9in (5411mm). **Width:** 6ft 2.3in(1887mm) over body, 6ft 7in (2008mm) over door mirrors. **Height:** 4ft 10.75in (1492mm). **Wheelbase:** standard cars, 10ft 0.5in (3061mm), long-wheelbase, 10ft 4.5in (3162mm). **Track:** 5ft 0.5in (1537mm).
PERFORMANCE & FUEL CONSUMPTION: 150mph, 0-60mph in 6.7 sec, 12-15mpg, 0-60mph in 6.3 sec with transient boost control.
PRODUCTION TOTALS: 4657 (standard saloon), 1508 (long-wheelbase).

Mulsanne S, 1987-1992

The Mulsanne S took over from the original Mulsanne as the core Bentley saloon model in October 1987 for the 1988 model-year. Although still very much the same car, it came with a package of changes that in most respects matched those on the contemporary Rolls-Royce Silver Spirit, and was immediately identifiable by its Mulsanne S boot lid badge.

Otherwise, the most obvious exterior change was to body-coloured housings for the door mirrors. On the inside, the Mulsanne S gained a stylish new centre console that reached from dashboard to floor in an unbroken sweep. It also took on a new

A 1989 Mulsanne S shows off its new spoked alloy wheels. (Charles01/CCA-SA 4.0)

dashboard, usually in straight-grain walnut, which incorporated the rev counter and 170mph speedometer from the Turbo R.

The 1989 models had twin round headlamps against a black background, a change made to all Bentley versions of the SZ for this year to reinforce the differences from the Rolls-Royce models. A headlamp power wash system also became standard, and Mulsanne S models destined for the US were all fitted with twin airbags – a specification that would not reach other markets until the 1994 model-year.

The 1990 Mulsanne S gained automatic ride control, and from July 1990 catalytic converters (already standard in the US and some other countries) became an option. The final cars were built with the new four-speed automatic gearbox that replaced the three-speed type, but there were relatively few of these. The gearbox change was introduced in January 1992, and Mulsanne S production ended in April, when the car was replaced in Bentley showrooms by the new Brooklands model.

MODELS: Four-door saloon, long-wheelbase saloon.
ENGINE: 6750cc V8 with 215bhp (estimated). 1987-1995 models with Bosch fuel injection. 1996 and later models with Zytek fuel injection.
GEARBOX: Three-speed GM400 automatic. Four-speed GM 4L80-E automatic from January 1992.
SUSPENSION, STEERING & BRAKES: Front suspension with coil springs, wishbones and anti-roll bar. Rear suspension with coil springs, semi-trailing arms, anti-roll bar, and high-pressure hydraulic self-levelling system. Power-assisted rack-and-pinion steering. Ventilated front disc brakes and solid rear disc brakes, with high-pressure hydraulic power assistance. Bosch ABS.
DIMENSIONS: Length: standard cars, 17ft 5in (5309mm), standard cars for US, 17ft 9.17in (5414mm), long-wheelbase (except US), 17ft 9in (5411mm). **Width:** 6ft 2.3in(1887mm) over body, 6ft 7in (2008mm) over door mirrors. **Height:** 4ft 10.75in (1492mm). **Wheelbase:** standard cars, 10 ft 0.5in (3061mm), long-wheelbase, 10ft 4.5in (3162mm). **Track:** 5ft 0.5in (1537mm).
PERFORMANCE & FUEL CONSUMPTION: 123mph, 0-60mph in 10.4 sec, 14-16mpg.
PRODUCTION TOTALS: 905 (standard saloon), 61 (long-wheelbase).

Brooklands, 1992-1998

From the 1993 model-year that began in October 1992, the core Bentley saloon was known as the Brooklands. It replaced both the Eight and the Mulsanne S, and could be had

The Brooklands entry-level model is seen here in 1994 guise. (Abxbay, CC by SA 4.0)

The long-wheelbase variant of the Mulsanne is exemplified by this 1995 Brooklands model. (Mr.choppers, CC-by-SA 3.0)

in both standard and long-wheelbase forms. Cars built in the first year of production were closely similar in specification to the Mulsanne S, but had their gear selector mounted on the centre console instead of the steering column, as pioneered on the Continental R models. They also had a new front air dam and a cleaner-looking bonnet with no central trim strip. The 1993 Brooklands cars would be the only ones with plate badges that had green enamel lettering.

The 1994 models had black badge lettering, and their wheel centre caps also had a black-enamelled centre badge instead of the B for Bentley on earlier wheels. On the mechanical side, the gearbox now came with the adaptive shift control system that adjusted shift points to suit the driver's style. Twin airbags – introduced four years earlier for the US – became standard for all countries, and there were redesigned seats with improved lumbar and lateral support.

All the SZ models had a major cosmetic makeover for the 1996 model-year. The Brooklands lost its quarter-lights, gained aerodynamic door mirrors and took on the redesigned front and rear bumpers and the shorter grille. Bumpers and sills became body-coloured, and a 16in version of the seven-spoke wheels from the Continental R became standard. Interior revisions included a new centre console layout. The switch to a Zytek engine management system brought around 6 per cent more torque, and the Brooklands now came with the taller final drive from the turbocharged cars, and a viscous-coupled differential as well.

The final revisions to the Brooklands model were made for the 1997 model-year, and the major change was switching to a light-pressure turbocharged engine that promised 300bhp and quite spritely acceleration. These and the 1998 models, which would be the last, also came with bright-finish alloy wheels. For the 1998 model-year, the Brooklands was accompanied by a Brooklands R variant, which is discussed separately on page 53.

As production of the SZ models drew to a close, some dealers gained factory permission to create their own special editions. The known ones (for which no sales figures are available) are the Indonesian Brooklands and the Trophy Edition Brooklands. These no doubt helped to keep sales up at a time when there was

The later spoked alloy wheels can be seen on this 1996-model Brooklands.

Later models of the SZ range had a centrally-mounted gear selector, as on this 1998 Brooklands.

already customer anticipation of the new Arnage models.

MODELS: Four-door saloon, long-wheelbase saloon.
ENGINE: 6750cc V8 with 238bhp (1992-1996,estimated). 6750cc turbocharged V8 with 300bhp (1996-1998). Bosch fuel injection (1992-1995). Zytek fuel injection (1996-1998).
GEARBOX: Four-speed GM 4L80-E automatic.
SUSPENSION, STEERING & BRAKES: Front suspension with coil springs, wishbones and anti-roll bar. Rear suspension with coil springs, semi-trailing arms, anti-roll bar, and high-pressure hydraulic self-levelling system. Power-assisted rack-and-pinion steering. Ventilated front disc brakes and solid rear disc brakes, with high-pressure hydraulic power assistance. Bosch ABS.
DIMENSIONS: Length: standard cars, 17ft 5in (5309mm), standard cars for US, 17ft 9.17in (5414mm), long-wheelbase (except US) 17ft 9in (5411mm) (except US). **Width:** 6ft 2.3in(1887mm) over body, 6ft 7in (2008mm) over door mirrors. **Height:** 4ft 10.75in (1492mm). **Wheelbase:** standard cars, 10 ft 0.5in (3061mm), long-wheelbase, 10ft 4.5in (3162mm). **Track:** 5ft 0.5in (1537mm).
PERFORMANCE & FUEL CONSUMPTION: 123mph, 0-60mph in 10.4 sec, 14-16mpg. Turbocharged models, 140mph, 0-60mph in 7.9 sec, 15mpg.
PRODUCTION TOTALS: 1429 (standard saloon), 190 (long-wheelbase).

Turbo S, 1994-1996

The ultra-high-performance Bentley Turbo S was released at the end of 1994 as a limited edition sold only in Europe (including the UK), Asia and the Middle East. The Turbo S was built only on the standard wheelbase and the original plan was to build no more than 100 examples; in practice, just 60 were made. It was perhaps as a result of this lower total that four 1995-model Turbo R cars were fitted with the Turbo S engine.

The Turbo S previewed some of the changes planned for the 1996 models, including those to the bumper and front air dam. Central to it was a new 402bhp version of the turbocharged V8 engine, which was also made available in the contemporary Continental S. This engine had a new management system developed by motor racing specialists Zytek in Britain, and had a water-to-air intercooler in place of the air-to-air type. The maximum speed was governed to 155mph (the figure agreed as a maximum in a European manufacturers' agreement) and the car came with a viscous limited-slip differential

The limited-volume Turbo S had different alloy wheels again.

as standard. It also had a new design of 17in seven-spoke alloy wheel.

MODEL: Four-door saloon.
ENGINE: 6750cc turbocharged V8 with 402bhp. Zytek engine management.
GEARBOX: Four-speed GM 4L80-E automatic.
SUSPENSION, STEERING & BRAKES: Front suspension with coil springs, wishbones and anti-roll bar. Rear suspension with coil springs, semi-trailing arms, anti-roll bar, and high-pressure hydraulic self-levelling system. Power-assisted rack-and-pinion steering. Ventilated front disc brakes and solid rear disc brakes, with high-pressure hydraulic power assistance. Bosch ABS.
DIMENSIONS: Length: 17ft 5in (5309mm), for US, 17ft 9.17in (5414mm). **Width:** 6ft 2.3in (1887mm) over body, 6ft 7in (2008mm) over door mirrors. **Height:** 4ft 10.75in (1492mm). **Wheelbase:** 10 ft 0.5in (3061mm). **Track:** 5ft 0.5in (1537mm).
PERFORMANCE & FUEL CONSUMPTION: 155mph (limited), 0-60 in 5.8 sec, 12-16mpg.
PRODUCTION TOTAL: 60.

Brooklands R, 1998

The Brooklands R was an upgraded performance-focused model of the earlier Brooklands that was made available for the final production season of the SZ range. It had the 300bhp light-pressure turbocharged engine and was distinguished visually by a mesh grille in place of the slatted type, by body-colour headlamp surrounds and by new bumpers with a black lower lip and black mesh inserts in the front air dam.

These cars also had the stiffer suspension and 17in wheels associated with the Turbo R, together with the high-performance braking system from the Continental T. The production run included 100 numbered examples of the Brooklands R Mulliner, which was prepared by Bentley's Mulliner bespoke division and came as standard with dark wood veneers, contrasting chrome instrument surrounds and other special interior features.

MODEL: Four-door saloon.
ENGINE: 6750cc turbocharged V8 with 300bhp. Zytek engine management.
GEARBOX: Four-speed GM 4L80-E automatic.
SUSPENSION, STEERING & BRAKES: Front suspension with coil springs, wishbones and anti-roll bar. Rear suspension with coil springs, semi-trailing arms, anti-roll bar, and high-pressure hydraulic self-levelling system. Power-assisted rack-and-pinion steering. Ventilated front disc brakes and solid rear disc brakes, with high-pressure hydraulic power assistance. Bosch ABS.
DIMENSIONS: Length: 17ft 5in (5309mm), for US, 17ft 9.17in (5414mm). **Width:** 6ft 2.3in (1887mm) over body, 6ft 7in (2008mm) over door mirrors. **Height:** 4ft 10.75in (1492mm). **Wheelbase:** standard cars, 10 ft 0.5in (3061mm), long-wheelbase, 10ft 4.5in (3162mm). **Track:** 5ft 0.5in (1537mm).
PERFORMANCE & FUEL CONSUMPTION: 140mph, 0-60mph in 7.9 sec, 15mpg.

The Turbo RT was the final version of the Mulsanne for 1997-1998.

PRODUCTION TOTALS: Overall total not known, but included 100 Brooklands R Mulliner models.

Turbo RT, 1997-1998

The Bentley Turbo RT was a special version of the Turbo R intended as a run-out edition. Although the factory always planned it as a long-wheelbase model, in practice small numbers of orders for standard-wheelbase Turbo RTs were honoured. There were also some limited-edition variants.

All Turbo RT models had the 400bhp Continental T powertrain, with Zytek injection and a single turbocharger. Maximum speed was limited to 150mph, at least partly to avoid overshadowing the recent Turbo S model. The RT had a mesh grille and colour-coded bumpers with bright mesh inserts, and came with distinctive five-spoke 17in alloy wheels sporting red centre caps.

For 1998, Bentley supplemented the Turbo RT with a limited-volume RT Mulliner, which, together with the contemporary Brooklands R Mulliner, heralded the company's use of the Mulliner name to indicate a bespoke specification. The RT Mulliner was available for special order only, and each one was individually built, some on the standard wheelbase.

The Mulliner car had an even more powerful engine – the 420bhp type from the latest Continental coupé with modified turbocharger and intake system – and a remapped management system. The cars had widened tracks and noticeably flared wheelarches to cover them. There were 18in wheels, and the bumpers were more rounded and aerodynamic than on the standard Turbo RT, with larger vents. A push-button starter and drilled pedals reinforced the sporting theme, and the black lacquer facia was matched by black leather door cappings. All headrests were embroidered with a winged B symbol, and the rear seats were electrically adjustable.

Multiple options reduced the risk of any two cars being identical. They included vents in the bonnet and front wings, a matrix grille, chrome wheels, door mirrors and headlamp surround panels, a smaller rear window and even a large white racing number roundel on the front doors. Wood finishes and machine-turned aluminium were offered instead of the standard interior black trim, and a speedometer for the rear passengers could also be fitted.

London dealer Jack Barclay gained permission to create a special edition in 1998 that took the name of RT Olympian. Among its features were the five-spoke alloy wheels from the RT Mulliner and an Olympian boot badge, but probably no more than four examples were ever made.

MODELS: Four-door saloon, long-wheelbase saloon.
ENGINE: 6750cc V8 with 420bhp. Zytek injection and single Garrett turbocharger.
GEARBOX: Four-speed GM 4L80-E automatic.

The Turbo RT Mulliner had a distinctive rear diffuser and, of course, identifying badges on the boot lid.

SUSPENSION, STEERING & BRAKES: Front suspension with coil springs, wishbones and anti-roll bar. Rear suspension with coil springs, semi-trailing arms, anti-roll bar, and high-pressure hydraulic self-levelling system. Power-assisted rack-and-pinion steering. Ventilated front disc brakes and solid rear disc brakes, with high-pressure hydraulic power assistance and Bosch ABS.
DIMENSIONS: Length: standard cars, 17ft 5in (5309mm), long-wheelbase, 17ft 9in (5411mm). **Width:** 6ft 2.3in (1887mm) over body, 6ft 7in (2008mm) over door mirrors. **Height:** 4ft 10.75in (1492mm). **Wheelbase:** standard cars, 10 ft 0.5in (3061mm), long-wheelbase, 10ft 4.5in (3162mm). **Track:** 5ft 0.5in (1537mm).
PERFORMANCE & FUEL CONSUMPTION: 150mph (limited), 0-60mph in 5.9 sec, 12-15mpg.
PRODUCTION TOTALS: 252 overall, consisting of 192 Turbo RT (2 standard wheelbase and 190 long-wheelbase), 56 Turbo RT Mulliner (7 standard wheelbase and 49 long-wheelbase), 4 RT Olympian. (Note that some authorities offer different figures.)

The body-colour grille surround and the alloy wheels indicate a Turbo R, the paired headlamps a 1989 or later model, and the number plate a US specification.

CONTINENTAL AND AZURE

The ultimate aim of the plan to re-establish the Bentley marque was to create a model not shared with Rolls-Royce, but that plan had to be accomplished in stages. The turbocharged V8 engine was a big step in the right direction, but it had to be used in a car that visually resembled its Rolls-Royce equivalent. Subtle distinctions such as the paired headlamps on 1989 Mulsanne models were a further help, but the real thing did not appear as the Bentley Continental R until 1991 – and even then it was based on the floorpan of the SZ range for reasons of cost.

The Continental R had its visual origins in a full-size concept model called Project 90 and displayed at the Geneva Show in March 1985. Designed by John Heffernan and Ken Greenley, both experienced car designers who had become tutors on the car design course at London's Royal College of Art, it was not specifically intended as a Bentley, but had fitted neatly into the future plans for the marque. A very enthusiastic public response confirmed thoughts that the design should be taken further.

Bentley's ambitious aim was to create a car in the mould of the legendary R-type Continental of 1952, and during 1986 the Project 90 shape was re-envisaged by Graham Hull in the styling department at Crewe with a striking, more angular theme. It offered all the necessary presence and prestige, and the gentle coke-bottle shape of its waistline hinted at the lines of the older Corniche coupé, to give a family resemblance. By early 1988 it had been turned into a full-size model and, in further modified form, the design was approved for production in November the same year.

Project 90 was the design concept that inspired the new Continental R.

Continental R, 1991-2002

The plan approved in November 1988 was to combine the new coupé body with the platform and running gear of the Turbo R.

The lines of Project 90 very much anticipated the production model, but were given greater definition in the Crewe styling studio.

The Continental R made its debut at the Geneva Show. This red example may be the show car itself.

So when the Continental R was announced at the Geneva Show in March 1991, it had the 333bhp turbocharged V8 engine, the four-speed GM automatic gearbox destined for other production cars later in the year, and the new electronic damper control system. New 16in five-spoke wheels completed the outside, while the interior pioneered a console-mounted gear selector (earlier cars always had it on the steering column). The show car was immediately bought by the Sultan of Brunei, and two years' worth of production had already been sold before customer deliveries began in early 1992.

Further development focused on the suspension, which was a little harsh, on giving the steering more feel, and on a traction control system that had not been ready in time for the first cars. The first major changes were tried on the Continental S limited-volume model in 1994 (which is discussed separately here), and some of that car's improvements found their way onto the 1996-model Continental R. This had the 385bhp Continental S engine allied to a taller final drive, a combination that not only reduced the 0-60mph time but also raised the top speed from 145mph to 151mph. In the meantime, the options were expanded by a convertible variant called the Azure and by the short-wheelbase Continental T model (both also discussed separately here).

Changes for the 1998 Continental R

Inside, the Continental R was a luxurious full four-seater, although rear legroom was not up to Bentley saloon standards.

The seven-spoke alloy wheels gave the low-production Continental S a more aggressive, sporty appearance.

were largely cosmetic, bringing a honeycomb mesh radiator grille in place of the earlier slatted type, and matching mesh grilles under the headlamps. The front seats were also reshaped and the upholstery style changed. From late 1999, the new Mulliner bespoke service became available for the Continental R, opening a wider range of personalisation to buyers – although it appears that only 46 Continental R Mulliner models were built between 1999 and the end of production in 2002. Beyond the cosmetics of paint and upholstery, a typical Continental R Mulliner might have the 420bhp Continental T engine, together with that car's stiffer suspension and larger 18in wheels.

The availability of the Mulliner bespoke service also enabled Bentley to build its own special variants of the Continental R, and two special editions followed. In 2000, the Millennium Edition of just ten cars had the wide wheelarches associated with the Continental T, a green starter button, a matrix grille and 18in wheels. In 2001, there were 131 Continental R Le Mans models, built to commemorate the marque's third place with the EXP8 car at Le Mans in spring 2001. These had the 420bhp engine, front wing vents, the wider wheelarches associated with the Continental T, a 'sports bumper' package,

The different frontal treatment marks this car out as a Continental R Mulliner.

Wing vents and wheels distinguished the Continental R 420. This is the first of just 18 made. (Akela NDE, CCA-SA 2.0)

red brake callipers in the fashion of the time, and four exhaust tailpipes. There were also special interior touches.

As production of the Continental R neared its end, several dealerships around the world produced special models, with the factory's approval. In alphabetical order, these were the Chatsworth Continental R, the Concours Beverley Hills Continental R, the Cornes Continental R, the Jack Barclay Continental R, the RSE Special Edition Continental R, the Stratton Continental R, and the Symbolic Continental R. Each one had its own special features. The ten Jack Barclay cars, for example, had flared wheelarches, 18in five-spoke wheels, a chromed radiator grille and surround, Azure-pattern seats with ruched leather and a turbo boost gauge.

MODELS: Coupé, Mulliner coupé, dealer special editions.
ENGINE: 6750cc turbocharged V8 with 333bhp (to 1995), 385bhp (from 1995) 400bhp (Continental T to 1997 and Continental SC) or 420bhp (Continental T from 1997). Bosch fuel injection 1991-1995; Zytek injection (from 1995).
GEARBOX: Four-speed GM 4L80-E automatic.
SUSPENSION, STEERING & BRAKES: Front suspension with coil springs, wishbones, automatically variable ride control and anti-roll bar. Rear suspension with coil springs, semi-trailing arms, dampers with automatically variable ride height control, and anti-roll bar. Power-assisted rack-and-pinion steering. Ventilated front disc brakes and solid rear disc brakes, with high-pressure hydraulic power assistance and ABS.
DIMENSIONS: Length: 17ft 6.5in (5346mm). **Width:** 6ft 11in (2058mm) over door mirrors. **Height:** 4ft 9.6in (1463mm). **Wheelbase:** 10ft 0.5in (3061mm). **Track:** 5ft 1in (1549mm).
PERFORMANCE & FUEL CONSUMPTION: 145mph, 0-60mph in 6.6 sec, 14mpg (1991), 151mpg, 0-60mph in 6.1 sec, 13mpg (1995).
PRODUCTION TOTALS: 1280 standard-wheelbase cars, plus 46 R Mulliner, 10 Continental R Millennium Edition, 131 Continental R Le Mans.

The interior of the Continental R incorporated all the latest Bentley sporting touches. (Matt5791, GNU Free Documentation Licence)

Continental S, 1994-1995

The Continental S was introduced in 1994 to increase interest in the Continental range and to explore ways it might develop. It was available for one year only, and only in certain European, Asian and Middle Eastern countries.

The primary feature of the Continental S was extra performance from a further-developed engine with an air-to-water intercooler for the turbocharger. This 385bhp V8 had been developed by Cosworth Engineering (who belonged to the Vickers Group that owned the Bentley and Rolls-Royce marques) and had modifications to the cylinder heads and induction system. It also had a Zytek engine management system in place of the earlier Bosch type. The revised engine was allied to taller final drive gearing to increase the top speed, although this was electronically limited to 155mph.

Just 39 examples of the Continental S were built, of which 21 had RHD. They proved the worth of the revised engine, which subsequently became standard on the further upgraded Continental R for the 1996 model-year.

MODEL: Coupé.
ENGINE: 6750cc turbocharged V8 with 385bhp. Zytek injection.
GEARBOX: Four-speed GM 4L80-E automatic.
SUSPENSION, STEERING & BRAKES: Front suspension with coil springs, wishbones, automatically variable ride control and anti-roll bar. Rear suspension with coil springs, semi-trailing arms, dampers with automatically variable ride height control, and anti-roll bar. Power-assisted rack-and-pinion steering. Ventilated front disc brakes and solid rear disc brakes, with high-pressure hydraulic power assistance and ABS.
DIMENSIONS: Length: 17ft 6.5in (5346mm). **Width:** 6ft 11in (2058mm) over door mirrors. **Height:** 4ft 9.6in (1463mm). **Wheelbase:** 10ft 0.5in (3061mm). **Track:** 5ft 1in (1549mm).
PERFORMANCE & FUEL CONSUMPTION: 155mph, 0-60mph in 6.1 sec, 13mpg.
PRODUCTION TOTAL: 39.

Azure, 1995-2003

The Bentley Azure was the convertible derivative of the Continental R, and its role was to replace the existing Bentley Continental convertible which had started life as a derivative of the SY (Bentley T Series) range in 1967. Development lasted from 1993 to 1995, and the model was announced in March 1995, its name chosen to give it an identity separate from that of its Continental R parent. The two cars shared the latest 385bhp version of the 6.7-litre turbocharged V8 engine, which in the Azure was governed to 150mph.

The Azure's body structure was developed with assistance from Pininfarina,

The Azure convertible admirably fulfilled its role of replacing the 29-year-old Continental type.

The shape of the Azure's lower body was shared with the Brooklands coupé. Right: Careful design of the folding top ensured the Azure looked as good closed as in open form.

and the Italian design house would retain an involvement with the car throughout its production life, undertaking partial construction of the bodies. The Continental R underframe was heavily reinforced to compensate for the torsional rigidity lost with the removal of the fixed roof, and Bentley claimed the Azure's static torsional rigidity was 25 per cent better than that of the Continental convertible it replaced. Even so, suspension settings were noticeably softer than for the fixed-roof cars, to preserve ride quality.

The lines of the convertible body were very much those of the Continental R, but the boot was raised very slightly to blend more smoothly with the rigid hood cover behind the rear seats, and the windscreen was not only more steeply raked than its coupé equivalent but also had thicker pillars to take the weight

The Azure interior was again an expression of contemporary luxury.

Wing vents and special wheels were among the identifying features of the Azure Final Series, as seen below.

The rear view of the Azure was also finely resolved. This is a Final Series car.

There were several differences from earlier cars in the interior of the Final Series, with the gear selector and the arrangement of the minor dials being clear here.

of the car in a rollover accident. The roof was, of course, power-operated, but space restrictions dictated use of a Perspex rear window, and the front seats with their integral safety belts were derived from those used in the BMW 850 coupé.

The production process of the Azure was complicated and took around 15 weeks. Floorpans made by the Rover Group at the former Pressed Steel works in Cowley went to Park Sheet Metal in Coventry, which mounted the front section of the car as far back as the B-pillars. These assemblies were then shipped to Pininfarina in Turin, where the rear body panels and the mechanism for the convertible top were fitted. The bodyshells subsequently returned to Crewe for paint and final assembly.

A Mulliner bespoke option was announced for the Azure in 1999, and was centred on the latest 420bhp engine, which was typically accompanied by front wing power vents. The car's final years included a Jack Barclay limited edition of ten cars to celebrate the dealership's 70th anniversary, called the Jack Barclay Platinum Anniversary Azure and featuring ruched leather and special 'starburst' walnut veneers. A special run of 62 Final Series models closed production in 2004, and these cars featured several options from the Mulliner programme plus a chrome-plated radiator shell which recalled the days before painted shells had taken over at Bentley.

MODELS: Drop-head coupé, Mulliner drop-head coupé, special editions.
ENGINE: 6750cc turbocharged V8 with 385bhp or (Mulliner models) 420bhp. Zytek injection.
GEARBOX: Four-speed GM 4L80-E automatic.
SUSPENSION, STEERING & BRAKES: Front suspension with coil springs, wishbones, automatically variable ride control and anti-roll bar. Rear suspension with coil springs, semi-trailing arms, dampers with automatically variable ride height control, and anti-roll bar. Power-assisted rack-and-pinion steering. Ventilated front disc brakes and solid rear disc brakes, with high-pressure hydraulic power assistance and ABS.
DIMENSIONS: Length: 17ft 6.3in (5342mm). **Width:** 6ft 11in (2058mm) over door mirrors. **Height:** 4ft 9.6in (1463mm). **Wheelbase:** 10ft 0.5in (3061mm). **Track:** 5ft 1in (1549mm).
PERFORMANCE & FUEL CONSUMPTION: 150mph, 0-60mph in 6.3 sec, 15mpg (1995 models).
PRODUCTION TOTAL: 1403.

Continental T, 1996-2002

The Continental T was a short-wheelbase, lighter and more sporty derivative of the Continental R announced in summer 1996 as a 1997 model. The wheelbase was

Wide wheelarches contributed to the muscular look of the short-wheelbase Continental T coupé.

Turned aluminium panels were a feature of the Continental T's dashboard.

This bright yellow Continental T showcased the Mulliner range at the Motor Show in Birmingham.

This knurled effect on the exterior door handle was among the Mulliner options.

Special interior features would become a Mulliner speciality; this diamond-quilted seating was on the Birmingham Continental T show car.

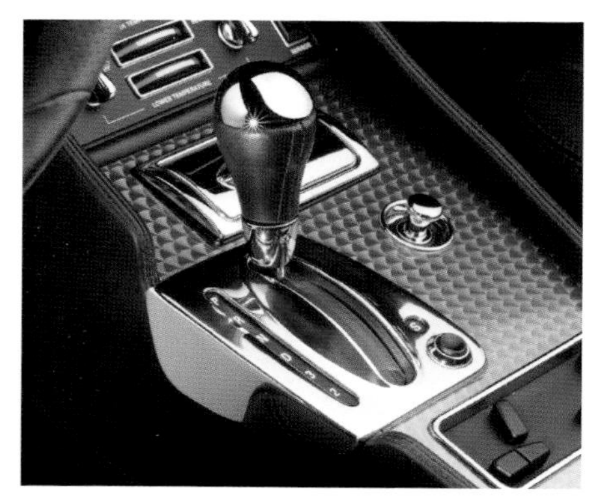

Left: The Continental T introduced a new arrangement for the gear selector.

The Mulliner cars were promoted as 'Personal Commission' types. This Continental T shows some of the exterior options.

The Mulliner options ensured that no two cars ever need be exactly alike. This is again a Continental T.

More Mulliner options: this specially crafted fitted luggage set for the Continental T was also displayed in Detroit.

reduced by 100mm (4in) to give more nimble handling, and the turbocharged 6.7-litre V8 engine was further developed to give 400bhp on the first cars. After the model had been on sale for about a year, further engine development delivered a significant torque increase, improving acceleration and flexibility. Its new peak of 650lb ft (875Nm) was more than any other production car engine in the world at the time.

The performance of the Continental T was matched by 18in wheels with 45-section tyres and new front brake discs made of micro-alloy. An electronic traction control system was available, and operated through the ABS sensors. Maximum speed was electronically limited to the 155mph adopted by consent among German manufacturers, and the 0-60mph acceleration time was just under 6 seconds. The interior featured engine-turned aluminium instead of wood for the dashboard and door cappings, in a deliberate evocation of the racing Bentleys from the 1920s.

Changes for the 1998 models centred on a power increase to 420bhp; the speed restrictor was removed and the top speed increased to 170mph while the 0-60mph time fell to 5.5 seconds. Like the Continental R, the Continental T gained a honeycomb mesh radiator grille in place of the earlier slatted

This Continental T Mulliner Personal Commission, with special wing vents, was displayed at the 2001 Detroit Motor Show.

Another Mulliner Personal Commission on the Continental T retained standard front wings without vents.

type, and matching mesh grilles under the headlamps. On the inside, the engine-turned panels gave way to a more conventional treatment, but sporty-looking drilled aluminium pedals were added, together with a chrome-plated gear selector lever and lever surround. The front seats were also reshaped and the upholstery style changed.

As was the case for the longer-wheelbase versions of the Continental, there were some special variants of the Continental T in its later years. The availability of the Mulliner bespoke service was announced in 1999 (and an eye-catching yellow car was displayed at the 2001 Birmingham Motor Show), and in 2001 a Le Mans specification celebrated the marque's third place at Le Mans with the EXP8 car. There was also at least one dealer special edition: the Chatsworth Continental T.

MODELS: Coupé, Mulliner coupé, special editions.

The quilted interior treatment could be extended to the rear luggage compartment of the Continental T.

ENGINE: 6750cc turbocharged V8 with 400bhp (to 1997) or 420bhp (from 1997). Zytek injection.
GEARBOX: Four-speed GM 4L80-E automatic.
SUSPENSION, STEERING & BRAKES: Front suspension with coil springs, wishbones, automatically variable ride control and anti-roll bar. Rear suspension with coil springs, semi-trailing arms, dampers with automatically variable ride height control, and anti-roll bar. Power-assisted rack-and-pinion steering. Ventilated front disc brakes and solid rear disc brakes, with high-pressure hydraulic power assistance and ABS.
DIMENSIONS: Length: 17ft 2.3in (5241mm). **Width:** 6ft 11in (2058mm) over door mirrors. **Height:** 4ft 6.9in (1447mm). **Wheelbase:** 9ft 8.5in (2959mm). **Track:** 5ft 1in (1549mm).
PERFORMANCE & FUEL CONSUMPTION: 155mph, 0-60mph in 5.8 sec, 14mpg (400bhp models), 170mph, 0-60mph in 5.5 sec, 15.1mpg (420bhp models).
PRODUCTION TOTALS: 322 Continental T, 23 Continental T Mulliner, 5 Continental T Le Mans.

Continental SC, 1998-2000

The Continental SC was a targa-top version of the short-wheelbase Continental T that had the 400bhp Continental R engine rather than the 420bhp type of the Continental T itself. The underframe was reinforced in a way similar to that of the Azure to compensate for the absence of a solid roof.

The Continental SC was a very special targa-roof derivative of the short-wheelbase Continental T.

The SC name stood for sedanca coupé, a body style that had been popular on Bentleys of the 1930s, although the only real parallel was in the ability to remove the roof over the front seats. The fixed rear roof section of the SC incorporated a darkened glass panel, and two matching darkened glass panels over the front seats could be lifted out and stowed under the boot floor.

Pininfarina had been engaged to assist in the development of the body, and both wings and bumpers differed slightly from those of the Continental T. A more aggressive front air dam contained extra driving lamps, and the sills were heavily flared. The SC had new 18in five-spoke alloy wheels, which could be ordered with chrome plating. It had the latest drilled pedals as standard, and the upholstery had the latest style of curved panelling. Top speed was governed to 155mph and the cars had slightly softer suspension than the Continental T.

All models of the SC had red lettering on their badges. As the most expensive production Bentley yet, they were never very numerous, and only 25 were built with RHD. Some of the later examples were built as SC Mulliner models with special features from the custom programme.

MODELS: Sedanca coupé, Mulliner sedanca coupé.
ENGINE: 6750cc turbocharged V8 with 400bhp. Zytek injection.
GEARBOX: Four-speed GM 4L80-E automatic.
SUSPENSION, STEERING & BRAKES: Front suspension with coil springs, wishbones, automatically variable ride control and anti-roll bar. Rear suspension with coil springs, semi-trailing arms, dampers with automatically variable ride height control, and anti-roll bar. Power-assisted rack-and-pinion steering. Ventilated front disc brakes and solid rear disc brakes, with high-pressure hydraulic power assistance and ABS.
DIMENSIONS: Length: 17ft 2.3in (5241mm). **Width:** 6ft 11in (2058mm) over door mirrors. **Height:** 4ft 9in (1460mm). **Wheelbase:** 9ft 8.5in (2959mm). **Track:** 5ft 1in (1549mm).
PERFORMANCE & FUEL CONSUMPTION: 155mph, 0-60mph in 6.1 sec, 14mpg.
PRODUCTION TOTAL: 73, including SC Mulliner models.

MODERN SPECIALS

Individualisation has been associated with the Bentley marque since its origins in 1919. The company has always produced the basic vehicle – in the beginning, just the chassis – and the customer has arranged for the car to be completed to their personal taste. Sometimes, the individualisation has been nothing more than a special upholstery or paint colour. The establishment of the Mulliner division in the late 1990s was intended to provide an in-house facility to enable all the work to be carried out in one place, which was convenient for the customer and also ensured Bentley could retain the associated profit and keep some control over what was done.

In the days of the separate-chassis cars, several coachbuilders provided coachwork to meet individual tastes, but the cost of this became prohibitive in the monocoque era. A few wealthy customers nevertheless commissioned conversions from aftermarket specialists, typically such things as estate cars. More radical, custom-built Bentleys did not disappear altogether, but were commissioned only by the exceptionally wealthy, and the outstanding figure among those was the Sultan of Brunei.

Bentley itself also constructed some interesting prototypes that were never translated into full-production models, and in fact one of them – the Java – became the basis of a series of cars built for the Brunei royal family.

Java, 1994

Crewe had been considering the possibility of a second and less expensive model-line for many years, and by the early 1990s these ideas became linked to the planned revival of the Bentley brand. The project was named Java (reviving a name used during the early 1960s for a model that did not enter production) and was intended to deliver a two-door model with convertible and coupé derivatives.

Design was subcontracted to DRA in Warwick and overseen by Crewe's own chief designer, Graham Hull. A BMW E34 (5 Series) underframe was used, and light weight was a high priority; the completed Java prototype weighed just 1725lb. The 6.75-litre V8 would have been overkill for such a car, and Cosworth Engineering – the Vickers subsidiary that had taken over production of the V8 engines when space at Crewe became too tight – was asked to prepare a suitable power unit. It did so by adding twin turbochargers to a 3.5-litre BMW V8.

The car was displayed in convertible form as a concept at the Geneva Motor Show in March 1994, and pictures released at the time also showed the hardtop coupé version. However, parent company Vickers decided against funding production of this new model-line, and the decision not to go ahead had

The Java concept car was an extremely attractive idea for a smaller Bentley, and was configured as a convertible.

The front end of the Java car retained a radiator grille that was recognisably Bentley, but the rest was more deliberately modern. (BLakerman, CC BY-SA 4.0)

The Java concept had a removable hardtop, which is seen in this rear view. (BLakerman, CC BY-SA 4.0)

probably been taken before the car appeared at Geneva.

Concept Java nevertheless aroused anticipation that there might be an exciting new Bentley on the way. The prototype was bought straight off the show stand by the Sultan of Brunei when he learned that it would not go into production. As explained below, he subsequently commissioned Bentley to build a whole series of copies, including coupé and estate derivatives.

Even though the Java car did not enter production, it was an important stage in the development of the Bentley marque, and its principles were absorbed into the strategy the Volkswagen Group adopted for Bentley when buying the company in 1998. It was therefore a distant and indirect ancestor of the 2003 Continental GT.

The Java interior maintained traditional levels of Bentley luxury.

The Jankel estates, 1989-1992

Robert Jankel Design was based in Weybridge and, between 1983 and 1989, had a contract to build the extended-wheelbase derivatives of the Rolls-Royce Silver Spur (which was essentially the same as a long-wheelbase Bentley Mulsanne). Under its own name, the company also built some bespoke conversions, such as two-door saloon versions of the Bentley Turbo R.

Jankel also built estate car conversions of the Turbo R, called the Val d'Isère on the standard wheelbase and the Provence on the long wheelbase. Both had a shortened rear overhang and one-piece tailgate hinged from the roof. The Val d'Isère had a four-wheel-drive transmission system that was optional on the Provence. Engaging Low or Reverse automatically engaged a hydraulic drive system that drove the front wheels through motors built into modified hub assemblies. The hydraulic pump that powered these motors was driven from the transmission by a toothed belt. At speeds above 30mph, the system disengaged automatically to return the car to normal rear-wheel drive mode. As explained below, several of the Val d'Isère estates were built for the Brunei royal family.

A unique estate

One 1983 Mulsanne Turbo was converted to an estate car when it was several years old by Coway at Westhoughton in Lancashire. It is thought to have remained unique.

Coway produced these plates to describe its car as a Shooting Brake.

This estate car conversion of a Mulsanne was done by Coway when the host car was several years old.

The side view of the Coway conversion was quite different from that of the Jankel estates.

The Brunei Bentleys

In the mid-1990s, Bentley created a series of very special cars for the royal family of Brunei. The Sultan and his brother, Prince Jefri, were avid car enthusiasts, and the royal collection amounted to thousands of cars. An agreement made probably in 1994 saw the company initiate a series of cars exclusively for the Sultan and his brother, mostly based on existing Bentley hardware. Between 240 and 250 of these special cars, which carried Bentley badges, were given type names of their own and had

A Jankel estate conversion from the early 1990s. Note the rear side window configuration.

special serial numbers from the sequence below 01001 at which standard production numbers begin.

It has been said that the patronage of the Brunei royal family was a major factor in keeping Rolls-Royce and Bentley afloat during this difficult period. What seems certain is that the development work done for the special Brunei cars fed into new production models, even if the Brunei cars themselves remained unavailable to other customers. In most cases, the cars were built in small batches, the smallest being of three cars and the largest consisting of 30.

Bentley itself has always maintained customer confidentiality and declined to provide any information about these cars or even to confirm their existence. Nevertheless, the cars are often seen in public on state occasions in Brunei, and some have even been kept and used in Britain. Over the years a group of dedicated researchers has identified large numbers of them, and it is important here to credit the work of Marinus Rijkers, which can be found at www.rrsilverspirit.com and underpins the comments here. However, many details still remain elusive, and the details in this book should therefore not be treated as definitive.

The earliest special cars for the Brunei royal family were delivered in 1989, and were examples of the Jankel Val d'Isère estate conversion. A total of 11 were supplied between then and 1992. As a next stage, the Italian coachbuilder Pininfarina was directly commissioned to convert a number of Continental R models.

There were two groups of these, each consisting of 13 cars. The design known as the B2 was a convertible that was also reskinned, and the cars were delivered between 1994 and 1996. The second group of cars had the B3 name, and these were coupés with the same outer panels that were delivered between 1994 and 1995. Pininfarina subcontracted the construction of at least some of these cars to Coggiola, a specialist prototype builder in Beinasco, near Turin.

All these early cars had standard VINs because they were converted from standard production cars. However, at some point in 1994, Bentley itself agreed to produce bespoke designs exclusively for the Brunei royal family. The first of these was a batch of 14 Continental R models with a special version of the turbocharged 6.75-litre engine that developed 527bhp and gave the cars a 0-60mph time of 5.0 seconds. These were known as the Sufacon cars, derived from SUper FAst CONtinental, and their engines had no catalytic converter and were known within the Bentley works as the Sultan-spec type or, more officially, by the code name of Blackpool. These cars were delivered in 1994. Some had standard VINs, but others were numbered in a special sequence that would be used for all the later Brunei specials.

Also delivered in 1994 were 12 Continental R convertibles, constructed by Pininfarina and retaining the basic lines

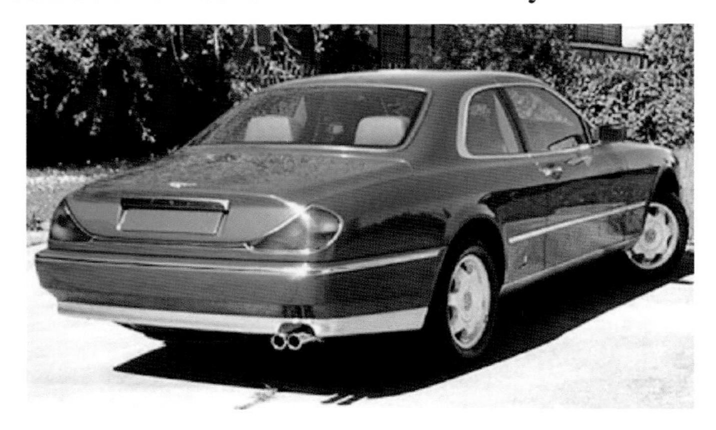

The Brunei specials are rarely caught on camera. This rear view shows the Pininfarina-designed B3 coupé.

of the original car. These anticipated the later production Azure convertible and had standard Continental R engines. An even more powerful version of the sultan-spec V8, with 542bhp, was used for three short-wheelbase Continental R models; the first was delivered in 1994 and was known as the Continental R Supershort, and the second pair, delivered in 1994 and 1995, were renamed Camelot. These three cars anticipated the production Continental T model.

Over the next three years, Bentley subcontracted aspects of design and build of the Brunei cars to a number of specialist companies, although it maintained tight control of each project. Design was entrusted to Pininfarina in Italy, and in Britain to two Coventry companies, Design Rights Associates and Geoff Matthews Design, and to Hawal Whiting Ltd in Basildon. Build was undertaken by several companies. Pininfarina built its own designs, and in the US both the American Sunroof Corporation in Detroit and Metalcrafters of Orange County in California became involved. In France, there was some work by Heuliez at Cérizay (and perhaps also by France Design at Le Pin). In Britain, cars were built by Hawal Whiting, MGA Developments in Coventry, Ricardo at Shoreham, RDS (Rig Design Services) at Southam, and by Motor Panels of Coventry (later known as Mayflower Vehicle Systems). All of these companies were established prototype and concept build specialists.

The remaining Brunei cars based on the Continental R were as follows:

1994-1997, Continental R Sports Estate: 30 cars. These were designed and built by Hawal Whiting. They all had the 527bhp engine, and six were armoured by Labbé in France.

1994-1995, Silverstone: eight cars. The Silverstone was a coupé-convertible with a retractable hardtop and the 527bhp engine. Designed by Hawal Whiting, the cars were built by the American Sunroof Corporation.

1995, Continental R Four-door: 19 cars. These were again designed and built by Hawal Whiting, and had the 527bhp engine.

1995, Continental R Long-wheelbase: 20 cars. These used the underframe of the long-wheelbase Mulsanne and had the 527bhp engine. Six were armoured by Manor Armour at Bridgwater, Somerset.

1995, Continental R Limousine: four cars. Styled by Geoff Matthews Design and built by MGA Developments, these had six-window bodies (with a short window and body section inserted between front and rear doors). They had naturally aspirated 6.75-litre V8 engines without catalytic converters.

1995, Monte Carlo: six cars. This was a GT convertible coupé on the Continental R underframe, which featured retro styling and a demountable roof. Design was by DRA, and build by Motor Panels.

1995, Imperial: six cars. Like the Monte

Carlo, this was a GT coupé with a demountable roof that was built on the Continental R underframe. The design was again by DRA, this time with a different 'retro' appearance, and the cars were again built by Motor Panels.

1995-1996, Spectre: nine cars. The Spectre was a convertible based on the Continental R, and was both designed and built by Pininfarina. The cars had the 527bhp V8 engine and, along with the contemporary Phoenix, were the first to have electronic traction control.

1995-1996, Phoenix: nine cars. The Phoenix was visually similar to the earlier B2 and, like that car, was designed and built by Pininfarina on a Continental R underframe. It differed in having the special 527bhp engine and, along with the Spectre, an ETC system.

1996, Highlander: six cars. This was a four-door GT with the 527bhp engine. It was designed by DRA and built in California by Metalcrafters.

1996, Buccaneer: six cars. The Buccaneer was a retro-styled two-door 2+2 sports coupé with the 527bhp V8 engine. Its headlamp design anticipated the style that Bentley adopted in the early 2000s. The car was designed by Geoff Matthews Design and built probably by Heuliez in France (but see the note above).

1996, Pegasus: 18 cars. These cars were built on a widened Continental R platform with the 527bhp engine, and there were six each of the coupé, convertible and estate variants. They were designed and built by Motor Panels and incorporated some visual similarities to the as-yet unreleased Arnage.

1996, Rapier: six cars. Built on a modified Continental R underframe, the Rapier was a two-door, four-seat sports coupé. Its design was by DRA and based on the Java, but these cars had the 542bhp engine of the Camelot. They were built by Hawal Whiting.

1996, Dominator: six cars. The Dominator was a remarkable exception even among the Brunei cars. It was a 4x4 based on the bodyshell of the contemporary second-generation Range Rover. The design was by DRA and the cars were built by RDS.

1997, Grand Prix: six cars. The Bentley Grand Prix was a radical design, two-seat sports coupé with a unique aluminium chassis and some body panels made of carbon fibre. Styling was done under Graham Hull at Crewe and the overall design came from Peter Hill, a Crewe development engineer. The V8-powered Grand Prix was supposedly capable of 190mph. The design dates to 1994, but the cars were probably not delivered until 1997.

As noted above, the Sultan was very taken with the Java show prototype, and bought the car when he discovered it was not going into production. He also commissioned a further 18 cars based on it, which were delivered between 1994 and 1996. The 18 were subdivided into six coupé, six convertible and six estate variants, with the estates built on a shortened wheelbase. Unlike the show car, they had twin-turbocharged 4.0-litre BMW V8 engines, possibly developed by Alpina in Germany. All were built by MGA Developments.

Another rare shot: this shows one of the Bentley Buccaneer bodies in build.

THE TRANSITION

The last years of the 20th century saw a major change for the Bentley marque when owners the Vickers Group put it up for sale along with the Rolls-Royce car division. A bidding war between two German car makers, BMW and Volkswagen, led to a period of transition in which BMW at one stage believed it had bought both marques; in the end, it did own Rolls-Royce, but Bentley went to the Volkswagen Group.

In the meantime, new models developed in the last years of Vickers' ownership went on sale – and these would be further developed under Volkswagen until that company had a range of all-new Bentley models ready.

Arnage (first series), 1998-2002

The production history of the Arnage saloon was profoundly affected by the changes in the ownership of Bentley Motors. The car was conceived in 1994 but was extensively reworked in the early 2000s under VW ownership. It was called the Arnage, after a corner at the Le Mans circuit where Bentley's sporting reputation had been forged in the 1920s.

Financial constraints obliged Crewe to buy in engines for the new saloons rather than develop a new one, and BMW became the chosen supplier. There was a V12 for the Rolls-Royce model (called the Silver Seraph), but the Bentley had a twin-turbocharged version of the M62 V8, further developed by Cosworth Engineering. That engine reached production with 350bhp, driving through the same five-speed ZF automatic gearbox that BMW used.

Body engineering was largely done by Mayflower, although the style was created by Graham Hull's team at Crewe. The suspension was mounted on separate subframes, and its basic design by Lotus was further developed at Crewe; the Bentley version was 40 per cent stiffer than the Rolls-Royce equivalent, and the Arnage also had bigger brakes and wheels to accommodate them. However, the engine and differential were mounted directly to the bodyshell, which was the first one to be manufactured completely at Crewe in an all-new body plant.

The Bentley Arnage was announced in June 1998, three months after its Rolls-Royce sibling. There were several visual differences between them, and the interiors were also different. At this stage, the Arnage came only with one wheelbase. There was some customer disappointment with the twin-turbo BMW engine, but the original model remained available into 2000. From 1999 it was renamed the Arnage Green Label (to distinguish it from the new Red Label model), and the final cars formed a limited edition of 52 called the Birkin Arnage.

Following current and anticipated trends in the motor industry, the Arnage was a visually smaller car than the model it replaced.

The red wheel centres mark this car out as a Red Label model. It is also a long-wheelbase variant, but the extra length in the rear doors is harder to detect.

When Volkswagen concluded the purchase of Bentley, it became clear that long-term use of the BMW engine was in jeopardy. Crewe's engineers had already done some preliminary work on installing their own 6.75-litre V8 into the Arnage, and Volkswagen agreed to fund further development of the engine rather than create a new one. As a first step, the existing 400bhp twin-turbocharged V8 was therefore introduced during 1999 in a new Arnage Red Label model alongside the BMW-engined cars, and this was equipped with bigger brakes and wheels. Both versions of the car also had newly stiffened bodyshells with relocated rear seats to improve passenger space, while park distance control and a pop-up satellite navigation system became standard.

The long-wheelbase Arnage went on sale in January 2001 after an autumn 2000 preview at the Paris Salon, and it came as standard with the 400bhp 6.75-litre V8. Three sizes were listed, with a 250mm (9.8in) stretch, a 450mm (17.7in) stretch, and a 728mm (28.7in) stretch, and all were available only to order and through the Mulliner division. The longest version had an extra body section inserted between front and rear doors, and both this and the intermediate 450mm-stretch car had their roofline raised by 100mm to maintain the good looks.

This is the standard-length Arnage in Red Label trim.

The 2002 model-year also brought an Arnage Le Mans Series to celebrate Bentley's return to the famous motor race. Based on the Red Label model, this had quad exhaust pipes, wing vents, wide wheelarches, 'sports' bumpers and five-spoke wheels. Among the special interior features were green instruments. It proved popular: 150 were planned but 153 were actually built.

MODELS: Arnage, Arnage long-wheelbase, Arnage Green Label, Arnage Red Label, Arnage Le Mans series, Arnage RL.
ENGINE: 4398cc V8 with 350bhp (Arnage and Arnage Green Label). Bosch injection and

This rear view of a Red Label saloon shows the attractive way in which all the lights now required had been incorporated, and how the boot lid was shaped to incorporate an aerodynamic spoiler. (pxhere.com – rights free)

two turbochargers. 6750cc V8 with 400bhp (Arnage Red Label). Bosch injection and single turbocharger.
GEARBOX: Five-speed ZF automatic (Arnage and Arnage Green Label). Four-speed GM 4L80-E automatic (Arnage Red Label).
SUSPENSION, STEERING & BRAKES: Front suspension with coil springs, twin wishbones, anti-roll bar and electro-hydraulic dampers. Rear suspension with coil springs, twin wishbones, anti-roll bar and electro-hydraulic dampers. Power-assisted rack-and-pinion steering. Ventilated disc brakes front and rear, with power assistance and ABS.
DIMENSIONS: Length: 17ft 8.2in (5389mm). **Width:** 6ft 4in (1930mm). **Height:** 4ft 11.6in (1514mm). **Wheelbase:** 10ft 2.6in (3116mm), Arnage long-wheelbase, 11ft 0.5in (3366mm), Arnage long-wheelbase option, 11ft 8.4in (3566mm), Arnage long-wheelbase option, 12ft 7.3in (3844mm).
PERFORMANCE & FUEL CONSUMPTION: 150mph, 0-60mph in 6.2 sec, 16mpg (Arnage and Arnage Green Label), 155mph, 0-60mph in 5.9 sec, 14mpg (Arnage Red Label).
PRODUCTION TOTALS: 3464, consisting of: 1123 (Arnage 1998-1999), 59 (Arnage Green Label, including 52 Arnage Birkin), 2282 (Arnage Red Label).

Arnage Series 2, 2002-2010

By autumn 2002, Bentley were ready with the re-engineered 6.75-litre V8, and this was introduced in October at the Detroit Motor Show, in the first of the Series 2 Arnage models. This was the higher-performance version, called the Arnage T, and came with 450bhp. It was followed in 2003 by the Arnage R with a 400bhp version of the engine and softer springing. The 'standard' long-wheelbase model became an Arnage RL.

The Arnage passenger cabin provided a cossetting feel to its passengers, as well as the traditional Bentley luxury.

The V8 engine had twin smaller turbochargers, modified cylinder heads, valves and exhaust manifolds, and revved higher than its forebears; it also had a Bosch management system that was readily compatible with other systems on the car. The Series 2 cars all had further stiffened bodyshells with a revised front air dam and a subtle boot spoiler and thicker sills. Inside, multiple changes were led by a new quilted diamond-pattern upholstery.

Though branded with the Bentley name, the engine under these cosmetic covers was in fact a twin-turbo BMW V8. (Flickr/The Car Spy)

The next new model was a special edition for 2004 called the Arnage T-24, built by the Mulliner division and promoting some more aggressive design features that supposedly linked it to Bentley's Le Mans race car. Basically an Arnage T, it had wing vents, polished split-rim wheels, four exhaust tips under a redesigned bumper, body-colour headlamp bezels and carbon fibre interior elements. The '24' referred to the Le Mans 24 Hours, and there were indeed 24 cars for the USA, plus a smaller number for Europe and the UK.

Determined not to be outdone by the latest Rolls-Royce Phantom, Bentley announced a reworked long-wheelbase car as a concept at the 2004 Geneva Show, and put it into production as the Arnage Limousine from January 2005; initial production was of 20 cars. It was based on the Arnage RL with its 250mm-wheelbase stretch, and was distinguished by 200mm-deep blind rear quarter panels. As on the other long-wheelbase models, all Limousines would be individually crafted by the Mulliner division, with the result that no two would be exactly alike.

A facelift gave all the 2005-model cars a closer resemblance to the Continental R through twin individual headlights and a raised bonnet line.

Later models had a modernised version of the long-standing 6.75-litre V8. This is in a Red Label car.

They also had uprated brakes and a refreshed interior with a better-integrated satellite navigation system. During 2006, a 60-strong Arnage Diamond Series celebrated 60 years since Bentley began postwar manufacture at

The Arnage T came with wing vents, special wheels and other distinctive features.

The 6.75-litre V8 in the Arnage T was 'signed' by the craftsman who built it.

Crewe. It had 19in alloy wheels, a stainless steel front bumper, Union Flag badges on the front wings and diamond inlays in the wood trim of the interior.

The 6.75-litre V8 was re-engineered again for 2007 to meet new emissions standards in Europe and the US, but power also increased: the Arnage R went to 456PS and the Arnage T to 507PS. Lightweight Mitsubishi turbochargers gave faster response, and on both models, the gearbox was changed for a six-speed type from ZF. A tyre pressure monitoring system also became standard.

There were no major changes for 2008, but in February that year a new 1100-watt Naim Audio sound system became optional across the range. Then in 2009 the Arnage Final Series celebrated ten years of the Arnage, 50 years of the V8 engine, and 90 years of the Bentley marque itself. The last of 150 examples were built in 2010, and this special edition combined the 507PS Arnage T engine with elements drawn from the contemporary Brooklands coupé. These cars had 20in five-spoke two-piece alloy wheels, dark-tinted upper and lower grille matrices, a retractable winged-B bonnet mascot, a 'jewel' aluminium fuel filler cap, and a 'Final Series' badge on each front wing. There were also some special interior touches.

Lights, grille and bumper apron were all developed over the years. This is a 2005 model Arnage Series 2.

Deeper rear quarters helped to maintain occupant privacy and the styling balance of the Arnage Limousine.

The Arnage Final Series of 150 cars celebrated several important anniversaries.

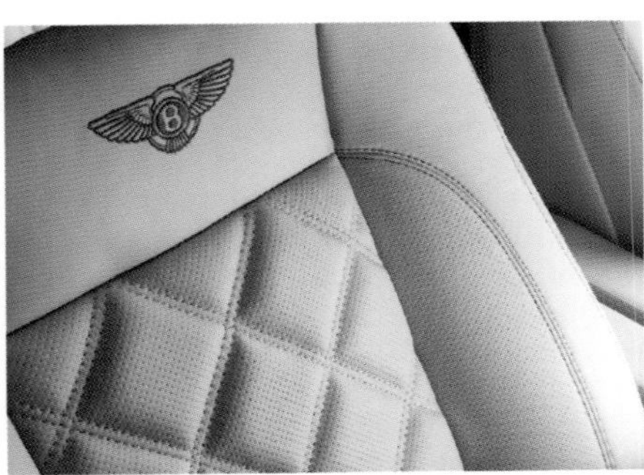

Bentley's much-liked diamond-quilted upholstery was a feature of the Final Series Arnage.

MODELS: Arnage T, Arnage R, Arnage RL, Arnage T-24, Arnage Limousine, Arnage Diamond Series.
ENGINE: 6750cc V8 with 400bhp (Arnage R to September 2006), 450bhp (Arnage T to September 2006), 456PS (Arnage R from September 2006) or 507PS (Arnage R from September 2006). Fuel injection and two turbochargers
GEARBOX: Four-speed GM 4L80-E automatic to August 2006. Six-speed ZF 6HP26 automatic from September 2006.
SUSPENSION, STEERING & BRAKES: Front suspension with coil springs, twin wishbones, anti-roll bar and electro-hydraulic dampers. Rear suspension with coil springs, twin wishbones, anti-roll bar and electro-hydraulic dampers. Power-assisted rack-and-pinion steering. Ventilated disc brakes front and rear, with power assistance and ABS.
DIMENSIONS: Length: 17ft 8.2in (5389mm). **Width:** 6ft 4in (1930mm). **Height:** 4ft 11.6in (1514mm). **Wheelbase:** 10ft 2.6in (3116mm), Arnage RL, 11ft 0.5in (3366mm), Arnage long-wheelbase option, 11ft 8.4in (3566mm), Arnage long-wheelbase option, 12ft 7.3in (3844mm).
PERFORMANCE & FUEL CONSUMPTION: 155mph, 0-60mph in 5.9 sec, 14mpg (Arnage R), 179mph, 0-60mph in 5.2 sec, 14mpg (Arnage T).
PRODUCTION TOTAL: 3840.

Project Hunaudières, 1999

Volkswagen had been exploring the possibilities for a mid-engined supercar since 1997, when it displayed its Synchro coupé concept, and as a next stage it presented a car with Bentley badges intended to determine whether the Bentley marque was the right home for such a car. This second car was called Project Hunaudières and was presented at the 1999 Geneva Show.

The Hunaudières concept car was put together around an existing mid-engined supercar from the Volkswagen stable – the all-wheel-drive Lamborghini Diablo VT – to save time and costs. Its new body was made

The Hunaudières concept explored a possible future for Bentley under Volkswagen. (Riceburner75, CC by-SA 2.0)

This press picture showed that the Hunaudières belonged to a modern sporting vision of the Bentley marque.

from aluminium and carbon fibre. Chromed lower body panels and chromed 20in wheels were designed to ensure the car looked good under the lights on the exhibition stand. The cabin was trimmed in typical Bentley fashion, with a combination of leather and aluminium, but looked to the future with dashboard screens that relayed the views from a pair of rear-facing cameras fitted behind the front wheels.

Bentley did not pursue the direction that the Hunaudières concept suggested, although the show car did have some influence on the eventual Bugatti Veyron from the Volkswagen Group. The engine of the Hunaudières nevertheless gave a strong hint of what might follow for production cars, and was a 623bhp 8-litre W16 related to Volkswagen's modular VR engine and created from two V8s. It drove all four wheels through a five-speed gearbox. The show car was also an early indication that new owners Volkswagen intended to mine the Bentley racing tradition. It was named after a straight section of the Le Mans circuit where Bentley had established its racing heritage, and it was painted in metallic British Racing Green.

MODEL: Concept car only.
ENGINE: 8004cc W16.
GEARBOX: Five-speed manual.
SUSPENSION, STEERING & BRAKES: Front suspension with coil springs and wishbones. Rear suspension with coil springs and wishbones. Recirculating ball steering with hydraulic power assistance. Disc brakes front and rear, ventilated and cross-drilled.
DIMENSIONS: Length: 14ft 3.5in (4430mm). **Width:** 6ft 6in (1980mm). **Height:** 3ft 10.8in (1190mm). Wheelbase: 8ft 8in (2650mm).
PERFORMANCE & FUEL CONSUMPTION: 220mph (350 km/h), 0-60mph 4.0 sec (estimated). No mpg figure available.
PRODUCTION TOTAL: 1 only.

Speed 8, 2001-2003

The Volkswagen Group decided that success at Le Mans would be of huge promotional value for their recently acquired Bentley marque, and during 2000 built the first version of a race car for the closed-cockpit LMGTP (Le Mans GT Prototype) class. Design and development were contracted to the British specialist RTN (Racing Technology Norfolk), which had also been responsible for the Audi racers already competing in the open-cockpit class.

The new car was known as the EXP Speed 8; EXP referred to its experimental status, while the Speed 8 designation recalled the Speed Six designation of the cars which had won Le Mans in 1929 and 1930, and indicated the new Bentley had an eight-cylinder engine. This was mounted longitudinally in the middle of the car, to give the best possible weight distribution. It was a development of the twin-turbocharged 3.6-litre engine that had powered Audi's 2000 Le Mans winner, and in the Bentley it drove through an Xtrac six-speed gearbox.

The car's monocoque body was made of carbon fibre and aluminium honeycomb to give maximum strength with minimum weight, and had a carbon rollover hoop integrated with the roof structure. Chassis and suspension were both developed from scratch, and weight was just 900kg. The first 'production' cars raced at Le Mans in 2001, and one of them came third behind two Audis and first in its class (in which it was the only entry).

For the 2002 season, the engine was further developed as a 4.0-litre with around 600bhp. Just one Bentley was entered that year, and after an almost trouble-free run, it finished in fourth place behind the three 'works' Audis. It also won the LMGTP class, for the same reason as in 2001.

The Audi team announced an end to

The EXP Speed 8 helped to remind the public that the Bentley marque had a history of sporting success.

The Speed 8 was further developed for 2003 – but it still looked nothing like any production Bentley model.

Success at Le Mans in 2003 brought the Bentley participation to a close, and Volkswagen went back to racing cars with Audi branding. As this picture shows, the Speed 8 had been quite extensively modified over its short career.

its racing activities in 2002 (although it did return to Le Mans a couple of years later), leaving the field open to Bentley. The car was extensively redesigned for the 2003 event, and was known simply as the Speed 8. It had new and more aerodynamic bodywork, and the twin-turbocharged V8 engine was re-engineered to meet the latest Le Mans regulations, finishing with 615bhp. Both suspension and gearbox were also revised.

Two of the new cars were entered in March for the Sebring 12-hour race in the USA, as a warm-up race, and finished in third and fourth places behind two Audis. There were also two entries for Le Mans itself, and these cars dominated the event from the start, finishing in first and second places. For the Bentley marque, it was a sixth Le Mans win, resuming the glory achieved in the 1920s. That, however, was enough. Bentley had earned the publicity, and now withdrew from Le Mans competition to make way for a return by its stablemate, Audi.

(Details below are for the 2003 Speed 8 cars.)

ENGINE: 4.0-litre twin-turbocharged V8 with 615bhp.
GEARBOX: Six-speed sequential manual gearbox.
SUSPENSION, STEERING & BRAKES: Front suspension with double wishbones, pushrods, torsion bar springs and telescopic dampers. Rear suspension with double wishbones, pushrods, torsion bar springs and telescopic dampers. Rack-and-pinion steering with electric power assistance. Ventilated carbon fibre discs on all four wheels, with six-piston AP Racing callipers.
DIMENSIONS: **Length:** 15ft 3in (4650mm). **Width:** 6ft 6.3in (1990mm). **Height:** 3ft 4in (990mm). **Wheelbase:** 107.9in (2740mm).
PERFORMANCE: Over 220mph. No further details available.
PRODUCTION TOTALS: Four to 2003 specification, plus six earlier cars.

The State Limousines, 2002

The largest Bentleys built in modern times were two identical custom-built State Limousines presented to Queen Elizabeth II for her Golden Jubilee in 2002. They were funded by a consortium of British Motor Industry manufacturers and suppliers, but design and manufacture was by Bentley at Crewe.

The running gear of the State Limousines was based on existing production Bentley hardware, the underframe being related to that of the Arnage RL and their engines being modified versions of the Arnage R's twin-turbocharged 400bhp 6.75-litre V8. Their front ends had a Bentley grille and other recognisably Bentley elements, but the bodies were entirely custom-designed and were manufactured by Bentley's Mulliner division. They had a high roofline with deep windows that allowed the monarch to be seen easily by the crowds on state occasions when she was riding in the car. The rear doors were hinged at the rear to provide maximum ease of entry and exit. Body and glass were armoured, and there was an airtight cabin sealing system to protect against gas attack.

Both cars were finished in the traditional royal claret, and carried a royal crest on the roof above the windscreen. The front compartment was upholstered in dark grey leather, with seats for the chauffeur and for a police protection officer. However, the rear compartment, which was used by the queen and other designated figures, was upholstered in a special light grey lambswool sateen cloth made in Britain.

MODEL: State Limousine.
ENGINE: 6750cc V8 with twin turbochargers and 400bhp.
GEARBOX: Four-speed GM 4L80-E automatic.
SUSPENSION, STEERING & BRAKES: Details not disclosed.
DIMENSIONS: Length: 20ft 5in (6220mm). **Width:** 6ft 6.7in (1999mm). **Height:** 5ft 9.6in (1768mm). **Wheelbase:** 12ft 9.5in (3946mm).
PERFORMANCE & FUEL CONSUMPTION: 130mph (210km/h). Other details not disclosed.
PRODUCTION TOTAL: 2.

The two State Limousines were unique creations for Queen Elizabeth II, and were delivered in 2002. (Bentley PR shot)
Less commonly seen is the rear view of a State Limousine. As is British tradition, neither car is identified by a registration plate. (S Foskett/GFDL)
Below is the interior of the State Limousine, optimised for short-distance parade work rather than long-distance travel. (BeBop 4, CC by-SA 3.0)

THE 21ST CENTURY CONTINENTAL

The new Bentley models designed under Volkswagen ownership opened a new era for the marque. Dimensions and power figures were now routinely quoted in the metric systems used in Germany (and, increasingly, in Britain). Inevitably, the cars shared some major components with the Volkswagen Group's other brands, although there was always something unique or special about the Bentley versions. The first model to be announced was the Continental GT coupé, in some ways a continuation of earlier thinking about a smaller Bentley, and deliberately intended to establish a strong performance image. Larger luxury saloons sharing much of that initial model's engineering soon followed.

Continental GT, 2003-2011

The Continental GT coupé was introduced in autumn 2003 and became the core model in a range that was gradually widened over the next decade. It was priced at around half the cost of the earlier Bentley Continental, bringing the marque to wider group of necessarily affluent buyers – a strategy that was rewarded with a massive increase in sales.

The new car was developed as the MSB (Mid-Size Bentley), and was considerably smaller than the 'full-size' Bentleys of the 1990s. Its all-steel platform was based on that of the Volkswagen Phaeton luxury saloon. It borrowed its sleek fastback coupé styling from the legendary R-type Continental of 1952, reinforced with 'haunches' that suggested an animal tensed and ready to spring. The front retained the twin headlamps and cross-hatched grille that had become Bentley trademarks.

The new coupé's engine was a Volkswagen W12, essentially two of the company's narrow-angle VR6 engines on a common crankshaft. With four banks of three cylinders each, it was relatively short, which allowed more space in the body to be used for the passenger cabin. The 6-litre Bentley W12 also had twin turbochargers and delivered 560PS (552bhp) in initial production form. Bentley chose a six-speed ZF automatic gearbox, which drove all four wheels through a Torsen (torque-sensing) centre differential with a 50-50 torque split that was automatically variable on demand.

Both the air suspension and its dampers had electronic control, and the interior was prepared to expected Bentley standards with leather upholstery and wood trims. It provided just enough room for four tall adults, and the dashboard featured a large information screen to control auxiliary functions, while keyless entry and keyless start were both made standard.

The Continental GT replaced the Continental R and Continental T models in the Bentley range. It exceeded its maker's predictions by 63 per cent when it attracted 3200 deposits at launch, and sold 5983 examples in its first year. This made it clear that Bentley exclusivity in the future would have to come from individualisation, as the volumes

The original Continental GT coupé presented the new face of Bentley. Despite some visual references to the legendary R Type Continental, it was really a new type of car. Perhaps the most striking feature of the styling was the pronounced 'haunches' at the rear.

The Continental GT interior combined modern supercar thinking with traditional Bentley touches.

The engine bay was beautifully presented, thanks largely to cosmetic covers over the W12 engine.

would far exceed the 1000 or so cars the old company had struggled to build in its final years.

Individualisation arrived in October 2004 with the optional Mulliner Driving Specification that brought 20in two-piece wheels with a seven-spoke design, plus diamond-quilted upholstery and other special interior features. By early 2006, Bentley was able to claim that 80 per cent of Continental GT buyers were new to the Bentley marque.

The Continental range was expanded in 2005 by the convertible GTC, in 2008 by Speed models, and in 2009 by Supersports models. All these are described separately here. Meanwhile, for 2007, the standard car took on the Flying Spur saloon's 19in, five-spoke alloy wheels and the four-door car's 20in seven-spoke type, with a choice of finishes becoming optional.

There were three special-edition variants of the Continental GT, beginning with the 2006 Diamond Series of 400 cars. These cars incorporated the Mulliner Driving Specification, plus unique tread plates and badges and a Mulliner alloy fuel filler cap. The Diamond Series also had carbon-ceramic brakes with black callipers and 14-spoke forged alloy wheels with a 20in diameter.

The second special edition was the Series 51 for the 2010 model-year, the '51' in the name recalling the year of 1951 when Crewe's own styling department was established by John Blatchley. There were both GT and GTC versions of the Series 51 cars, both focusing on new interior options. Two-tone paint was available, and all cars had special badges and 14-spoke polished Diamond wheels with dark centre caps.

The third special edition was the Continental GT Design Series China, announced as a 2011 model at the April 2010 Beijing Auto Show and available only for China, which had become Bentley's third-largest market globally. It had special badges and two unique colours (Orange Flame and Magenta Metallic) chosen to suit Chinese tastes.

MODELS: Continental GT, Continental GT Diamond Series, Continental GT Series 51, Continental GT Design Series China.
ENGINE: 5998cc W12 with 552bhp.
TRANSMISSION: ZF 6HP26 automatic. Four-wheel drive with Torsen centre differential.
SUSPENSION, STEERING & BRAKES: Front independent suspension with four-link double wishbones, computer-controlled self-levelling air springs and anti-roll bar. Rear independent suspension with trapezoidal multi-links, computer-controlled self-levelling air springs

The Design Series China was specially produced for that country, with unique paint colours.

and anti-roll bar. Continuous damping control with four adjustable settings. Servotronic speed-sensitive power-assisted rack-and-pinion steering. Ventilated disc brakes on all four wheels, with ABS.
DIMENSIONS: Length: 15ft 9.3in (4808mm), 2003-2005. 15ft 9.1in (4804mm), 2006-2011. **Width:** 6ft 3.5in (1918mm). **Height:** 4ft 6.7in (1390mm). **Wheelbase:** 9ft 0.1in (2746mm).
PERFORMANCE & FUEL CONSUMPTION: 197.6mph, 0-60mph in 4.8sec, 16-17mpg.
PRODUCTION TOTAL: 31,500 (estimated; all Continental GT, including GTC models).

Continental GTC, 2005-2011

The convertible version of the Continental GT was developed with the assistance of German specialist builder Karmann, which also took on manufacture of the car's complex, hydraulically-operated convertible roof assembly. The Continental GTC was announced in September 2005, but production did not begin until autumn 2006.

The sills of the GTC's body were reinforced, there was additional cross-bracing underneath the passenger cabin, and strengthened tubing was used to reinforce the windscreen pillars and windscreen surround. The rear suspension was modified to cope with the altered weight distribution, and changes to the steering reflected the modifications seen earlier in the year on the Flying Spur. The interior was broadly similar to that of the parent Continental GT, but the front seats had recessed backs to improve kneeroom in the rear. The standard Continental GTC had the same drivetrain as the contemporary Continental GT, but its extra weight and the drag of the convertible top made it slightly slower.

Like the Continental GT, the GTC was gradually developed over the years. From late 2009, a GTC Speed model became available,

This GTC presented the Series 51 models to good effect at the 2010 Geneva Show.

The GTC convertible came with the usual luxuriously appointed passenger compartment.

and is described below. Both the Speed model and the standard GTC for 2010 had front end changes that included a more upright grille.

From August 2010, limited '80-11' editions of the GTC and the GTC Speed were released in the US as 2011 models. Their name indicated there were 80 examples of each for the 2011 model-year, and both shared an all-black interior with piano black wood veneer, although there were subtle differences between them.

MODELS: Continental GTC, Continental GTC Speed, Continental GTC 80-11, Continental GTC Speed 80-11.
ENGINE: 5998cc W12 with 552bhp (GTC) or 600bhp (GTC Speed).
TRANSMISSION: ZF 6HP26 automatic. Four-wheel drive with Torsen centre differential.
SUSPENSION, STEERING & BRAKES: Front independent suspension with four-link double wishbones, computer-controlled self-levelling air springs and anti-roll bar. Rear independent suspension with trapezoidal multi-links, computer-controlled self-levelling air springs and anti-roll bar. Continuous damping control with four adjustable settings. Servotronic speed-sensitive power-assisted rack-and-pinion steering. Ventilated disc brakes on all four wheels, with ABS.
DIMENSIONS: Length: 17ft 4.94in (5307mm). **Width:** 6ft 3.5in (1918mm), 6ft 5.4in (1966mm), from 2009. **Height:** 4ft 6.7in (1390mm). **Wheelbase:** 9ft 0.07in (2745mm).
PERFORMANCE & FUEL CONSUMPTION: 195mph, 0-60mph in 4.8 sec, 17mpg (GTC). 200mph, 0-60mph in 4.8 sec, 17mpg (GTC Speed).
PRODUCTION TOTAL: 31,500 (estimated; all Continental GT, including GTC models).

With the top raised, the GTC retained its sleek appearance. This is another Series 51 car.

The Speed model was the next step up in performance, represented here by a GTC variant.

Continental GT and GTC Speed, 2008-2011

Speed models of the Continental GT and the convertible GTC were an inevitable progression. The GT was announced first, in August 2007 as a 2008 model, and the GTC followed in late 2009 as a 2010 model.

The Speed name harked back to the days of the 'WO' Bentleys, and was a simple indication that these models had higher performance than the standard cars that remained in production alongside them. The W12 engine was uprated to deliver 600PS (592bhp), with new pistons and conrods, better crankcase breathing and a new engine management system. In addition, the turbocharger boost was slightly increased, to give more torque all the way through the rev range. Speed models had a strengthened gearbox, firmer suspension and sharper steering, and the early GT was also 35kg (77lb) lighter than the standard coupé. They also had a discreet rear spoiler and lowered suspension to improve the handling, and the GTC variant became the first open Bentley to reach 200mph.

Bentley initially estimated the Speed model might take anywhere between 15 per cent and 50 per cent of Continental GT sales, but in practice the figure rapidly reached 70 per cent. This was a clear indication of what the customers wanted, and pointed the way to the next performance-enhanced model, which was released as the Supersports in 2009.

In 2007, Finnish rally ace and four-times World Rally Champion Juha Kankkunen used an early Bentley Continental GT Speed model to break the world speed record on ice.

MODELS: GT Speed, GTC Speed.
ENGINE: 5998cc W12 with 600bhp.
TRANSMISSION: ZF 6HP26 automatic gearbox. Four-wheel drive with Torsen centre differential.
SUSPENSION, STEERING & BRAKES: Front independent suspension with four-link double wishbones, computer-controlled self-levelling air springs and anti-roll bar. Rear independent suspension with trapezoidal multi-links, computer-controlled self-levelling air springs and anti-roll bar. Continuous damping control with four adjustable settings. Servotronic speed-sensitive power-assisted rack-and-pinion steering. Ventilated disc brakes on all four wheels, with ABS.
DIMENSIONS: Length: 17ft 4.94in (5307mm). **Width:** 6ft 3.5in (1918mm), 6ft 5.4in (1966mm), from 2009. **Height:** 4ft 6.3in (1380mm). **Wheelbase:** 9ft 0.07in (2745mm).
PERFORMANCE & FUEL CONSUMPTION: 202mph, 0-60mph in 4.3 sec, 17mpg.

PRODUCTION TOTAL: 31,500 (estimated; all Continental GT, including GTC models).

Continental Supersports, 2009-2011

The Continental Supersports models were not in the original product plan for the Continental GT, but came about when the engine development team achieved a new and higher 630PS tune for the W12 engine. The Supersports name was a borrowing from the Bentleys of the 1920s, when it was given to a high-performance, short-chassis version of the WO Bentley 3-litre.

The Supersports was announced at the March 2009 Geneva Show, and deliveries began that autumn, although there would be none for North America until summer 2010. All the first cars were coupés, but a Continental Supersports Convertible was added in April 2010.

The 630PS engine made the Supersports the fastest and most powerful production Bentley built to that point. From summer 2010, it was made capable of running on either petrol or E85 ethanol, in line with the new greener policies Bentley outlined in 2008. The engine was far from the only special feature, however: the gearbox had a Quickshift system that reduced shift times by 50 per cent and enabled double downshifts, and a revised Torsen centre differential split the torque differently, with 40 per cent now going to the front wheels and 60 per cent to the rears.

The Supersports had its own rather aggressive appearance, thanks to lowered suspension, a set of large air intakes and dark headlamp trim at the front, and wider rear wheelarches to accommodate a two-inch-wider track. Gloss black was used for the 20in alloys of a new design and for the window surrounds and lower body trim. The rear spoiler was unique, and there were smoked-glass rear lamps and a special lower rear apron around twin oval-shaped tailpipes.

Above: In coupé form, the Continental Supersports became the fastest and most powerful production Bentley built.

The Continental Supersports convertible joined the range in spring 2010.

The whole car was also 110kg lighter than its standard equivalent, over half of which was saved by reducing the cabin trim and fitting carbon fibre racing front seats with only a brace bar at the rear.

The suspension of the convertible versions was slightly softer than on the coupé, but these still sat around 10mm lower than a GTC Speed, and had tighter dampers and stiffer suspension bushes. In February 2011, Juha Kankkunen used a Supersports Convertible to break the ice driving record he had set in 2007 with a Continental GT Speed, raising his average speed to 205.48mph (330.695km/h).

MODELS: Supersports Coupé, Supersports Convertible.
ENGINE: 5998cc W12 with 630bhp.
TRANSMISSION: ZF 6HP26A incorporating 'Quickshift' mode. Four-wheel drive with Torsen centre differential.
SUSPENSION, STEERING & BRAKES: Front independent suspension with four-link double wishbones, computer-controlled self-levelling air springs and anti-roll bar. Rear independent suspension with trapezoidal multi-links, computer-controlled self-levelling air springs and anti-roll bar. Continuous damping control with four adjustable settings. Servotronic speed-sensitive power-assisted rack-and-pinion steering. Ventilated carbon/ceramic cross-drilled disc brakes on all four wheels, with ABS.
DIMENSIONS: Length: 17ft 4.94in (5307mm). **Width:** 6ft 4.6in (1946mm). **Height:** 4ft 6.3in (1380mm). **Wheelbase:** 9ft 0.07in (2745mm).
PERFORMANCE & FUEL CONSUMPTION: 204mph, 0-60mph in 3.7 sec, 17mpg.
PRODUCTION TOTAL: 31,500 (estimated; all Continental GT, including GTC models).

Continental GTZ, 2008-2010

The Continental GTZ was the first Bentley to be bodied by the Italian coachbuilder Zagato, and was limited to just nine examples. Some of these were converted from older GT Speed models, and two had RHD. The car was announced at the Geneva Show in March 2008, but that year's economic crash interrupted production at Zagato. It resumed in 2010.

The GTZ was immediately recognisable as a derivative of the Continental GT family, but in fact Zagato completely replaced the original body with one containing lightweight aluminium elements that reduced weight by around 100kg. Only the headlights remained from the original car. The rear wing 'haunches' were exaggerated and the roofline was restyled to feature the Italian company's trademark 'double-bubble' style. A lengthened tail featured new LED lights and reduced the rear window to a slit, so cameras and the dashboard screen were used to provide rearward vision. A two-tone paint scheme was part of the Zagato conversion. The interior remained broadly similar to the original, but the seats were reupholstered to feature a broad band running from top to bottom and containing the Zagato 'Z' motif.

Zagato's GTZ retained the overall shape of the Continental GT but treated it uniquely.

These were deliberately bespoke cars, and no two were exactly alike. One of the

The 'double-bubble' roof design had been associated with Zagato since the 1950s and originated as a means of improving aerodynamics in racing.

The GTZ also had its own bespoke interior treatment.

The GTZ cars were very much treated as bespoke creations, and this one for a UK owner had partially spatted rear wheels.

RHD cars for a UK customer was built to an individual specification with partially covered rear wheels.

Continental Flying Star, 2010

The Continental Flying Star was a shooting brake conversion of the Continental GT built by the Italian coachbuilder Carrozzeria Touring Superleggera. A single example was initially commissioned by a private client in 2008 and a limited edition of 19 cars was subsequently approved. The first complete car was displayed on the Touring Superleggera stand at Geneva in March 2010 and had standard 560PS engine, but Touring also offered the conversion for the 610PS Speed and 630PS Supersports models.

The conversion was based on the stiffer bodyshell of the Continental GTC, and Touring Superleggera created an entirely new body aft of the windscreen pillars. The roof was made of lightweight steel sheet with concealed steel support bars, and the doors and tailgate were made from aluminium. A flat load floor provided 400 litres of space with the rear seats in place but three times that when the seats were folded forward. Options included 20in Borrani cross-spoke wire wheels with a variety of finishes.

Continental GT, 2011-2018

The second-generation Continental GT was previewed at the Paris Motor Show in autumn 2010 but did not go on sale until a year

The Continental Flying Star was another special coachbuilt car, this time Touring Superleggera's vision of what a shooting brake could be.

The rear of the Flying Star blended perfectly with the original Bentley body shape.

The Flying Star's rear seats were designed to fold down to extend the load area.

later as a 2012 model. The 6.0-litre W12 engine now delivered 567bhp as against the 2011 model's 552bhp, thanks to some new low-friction features and reprogrammed electronics. Performance improved to deliver 0-60mph in 4.4 seconds and a 198mph top speed. The second-generation Continental GT was, of course, accompanied by a slightly slower Continental GTC with the same major changes.

The 40-60 split Torsen differential and the Quickshift gear-changing enhancement from the Supersports models became standard on both models. There were also wider tracks, and a new electronic stability control designed to keep the car more stable in high-speed corners.

The broad outline and major dimensions of the Continental remained unchanged, although the front end had been redesigned with new headlights, the inner pair being larger than the outers and featuring surrounding LEDs. The bonnet had been reshaped to appear more muscular and was actually longer than before thanks to a more upright and lower-mounted grille. Bentley had also achieved a cleaner appearance by eliminating the joint between the front wing and the bumper. At the rear, changes below the boot lid spoiler added the new double-horseshoe shape introduced on the new Mulsanne models.

Meanwhile, the passenger cabin had also been redesigned with a more curvaceous dashboard that incorporated a new touch screen and simpler satnav system. Redesigned seats were lighter and more supportive than before, and gave more rear legroom, while there were also larger door pockets.

Further development of these second-generation models would follow the same lines as that of the earlier cars, with Speed and Supersports models being added later; both types are discussed separately below. However, a major departure for the range was the introduction of an alternative V8 engine in 2012, which is also discussed below.

Running changes included the arrival of a series of equipment packages for the 2014 model-year. These included an interior style specification that focused on an individualised and hand-created passenger cabin, and a premier specification that brought additional technology and comfort features. There were further updates at the Geneva Show in 2015, and deliveries of these revised cars began in the summer.

At this stage, the W12 took on a cylinder deactivation system like that pioneered on the V8 models (see below), which shut off six cylinders at cruising speeds. Its power output was also increased to 582bhp (590 PS) and torque to 531lb ft (720Nm). There were several cosmetic changes, too: the front gained a new bumper and a smaller radiator shell, while the wings incorporated new vents and carried new badges. At the rear, the boot lid was redesigned and there was a new rear bumper with full-width bright trim. New wheels in both standard 20in and optional 21in sizes were introduced. On the inside, the upholstery could be ordered in semi-aniline leather, and there was a new storage and device-charging compartment between the rear seats. The dashboard, instruments and controls also underwent multiple changes.

A further special edition was released in 2016 as the Continental GT Speed Black

Headlamps of different sizes were the easiest way of recognising the second-generation Continental GT.

Edition, with similar styling enhancements to those on the contemporary Flying Spur Black edition (see below). These cars had metallic anthracite grey paintwork, with black upholstery and cyber yellow for highlights on the body and the seats.

The second-generation Continental GT range remained in production until 2018, when they were all replaced by a third-generation series of cars.

MODELS: GT Coupé, GTC Convertible.
ENGINE: 5998cc W12 with 567bhp.
TRANSMISSION: ZF 8HP90 incorporating 'Quickshift' mode. Four-wheel drive with Torsen centre differential.
SUSPENSION, STEERING & BRAKES: Front independent suspension with four-link double wishbones, computer-controlled self-levelling air springs and anti-roll bar. Rear independent suspension with trapezoidal multi-links, computer-controlled self-levelling air springs and anti-roll bar. Continuous damping control with four adjustable settings. Servotronic speed-sensitive power-assisted rack-and-pinion steering. Ventilated carbon/ceramic cross-drilled disc brakes on all four wheels, with ABS.
DIMENSIONS: Length: 17ft 4.94in (5307mm). **Width:** 6ft 4.6in (1946mm). **Height:** 4ft 6.3in (1380mm). **Wheelbase:** 9ft 0.07in (2745mm).
PERFORMANCE & FUEL CONSUMPTION: 204mph, 0-60mph in 3.7 sec, 17mpg.
PRODUCTION TOTAL: 42,225 (estimated; all Continental GT and GTC).

Continental GT (V8), 2012-2018

A companion V8-powered variant of the second-generation Continental GT was introduced at the Detroit Show in January 2012 and went on sale in the spring. The same engine was made available for the GTC. The engine was a variant of the latest Audi 4.0-litre engine, with a unique 500bhp tune and featuring twin turbochargers, direct fuel injection and fuel-saving cylinder deactivation at cruising speeds, when four cylinders automatically became inactive. The new engine came with a new eight-speed automatic gearbox and resulted in a car that was not much slower than the W12 model, but was considerably less expensive to buy and run, and, as some commentators suggested, had a more overtly sporting feel.

The V8 models came with 20in wheels as standard, with a 21in option. The cars had a red background for the badges on the bonnet boot and wheel centres. They also had a three-piece front bumper and a gloss black grille with a chrome frame and central bar. The rear end differed from the W12 models through chromed figure-of-eight exhaust tailpipes and a dark lower valance.

MODELS: GT Coupé, GTC Convertible.
ENGINE: 3993cc twin-turbocharged V8 with 500bhp.
TRANSMISSION: ZF eight-speed automatic. Four-wheel drive with Torsen centre differential.
SUSPENSION, STEERING & BRAKES: Front independent suspension with four-link double wishbones, computer-controlled self-levelling air springs and anti-roll bar. Rear independent suspension with trapezoidal multi-links, computer-controlled self-levelling air springs and anti-roll bar. Continuous damping control with four adjustable settings. Servotronic speed-sensitive power-assisted rack-and-pinion steering. Ventilated carbon/ceramic cross-drilled disc brakes on all four wheels, with ABS.
DIMENSIONS: Length: 17ft 4.94in (5307mm). **Width:** 6ft 4.6in (1946mm). **Height:** 4ft 6.3in (1380mm). **Wheelbase:** 9ft 0.07in (2745mm).
PERFORMANCE & FUEL CONSUMPTION: 190mph (GTC 187mph), 0-60mph in 4.6 sec (GTC 4.7 sec), 24mpg.
PRODUCTION TOTAL: 42,225 (estimated; all Continental GT and GTC).

A gloss black grille and redesigned front details mark this out as a V8 S model of the Continental GT.

Le Mans Edition, 2013

For the US market, Bentley produced a Le Mans Edition that went on sale alongside the Mulsanne Le Mans edition in late 2013. Buyers chose from one of six appearance packages named after the drivers of the six Le Mans-winning Bentleys. Both coupé and convertible types were on offer. Each package was limited to 48 cars (made up of both Continental and Mulsanne versions) and were named after John Duff (the 1924 winner), Dudley Benjafield (1927), Woolf Barnato (1928), Tim Birkin (1929), Glen Kidston (1930) and Guy Smith (2003).

The cars had the 567bhp V12 engine and 21in seven-spoke wheels in black with machined faces, while the wings carried Le Mans Edition badges. There were special exterior colour schemes, and the interior features included specially embroidered headrests and numbered special-edition plaques.

PRODUCTION TOTAL: 288 cars, including Mulsanne variants; individual totals not available.

Continental GT Speed models, 2014-2018

Bentley announced the Speed version of its second-generation Continental GT in two stages. The coupé model made its first appearance at the Goodwood Festival of Speed in June 2014, and the convertible was introduced at the Detroit Show in January 2015.

For the Speed models, the W12 engine gained a new management system and power went up to 616bhp (625PS), with 590lb ft (800Nm) of torque. Top speed increased to 205mph (330km/h) and the 0-60mph time dropped to 4.0 seconds; convertibles were slightly slower than the coupés. A sports suspension was standard, set 10mm lower than the standard cars and featuring uprated anti-roll bars, air springs and dampers. The Mulliner Driver's Specification was also standard.

There were 21in alloy wheels as standard, with a choice between silver and a dark tint. Electronic stability control with dynamic mode was standard. Cosmetic distinction came from a matrix radiator grille and bumper air intakes with a dark-tinted chrome finish, and both front wings carried chrome 'Speed' badges. The interior had diamond-quilted leather upholstery and dark tint aluminium 'engine spin' finish, with the options of fine wood veneers and a satin-finish carbon fibre option for the dashboard and centre console.

Further revisions for the 2015 model-year brought engine power up to 627bhp (635PS) and torque to 810Nm (596lb ft). Also new was a bodykit that consisted of a front splitter, side skirts and a rear diffuser. The dark tint 21in wheels became standard, front and rear lamp lenses were given a dark tint, and there was a choice of red or black brake callipers. Inside, the dashboard gained a Speed badge and there was a new and unique colour split. More changes were made to the interior for the 2016 model-year, following the same pattern as on the standard GT models but adding a straight-fluted design with a small-diamond pattern.

MODELS: GT Speed Coupé, GTC Speed Convertible.
ENGINE: 5998cc W12 with 616bhp; 627bhp from 2015.

The GT3-R was a roadgoing version of the Continental GT3 competition cars. (©More Cars, CCA 2.0)

TRANSMISSION: ZF 6HP26A incorporating 'Quickshift' model. Four-wheel drive with Torsen centre differential.
SUSPENSION, STEERING & BRAKES: Front independent suspension with four-link double wishbones, computer-controlled self-levelling air springs and anti-roll bar. Rear independent suspension with trapezoidal multi-links, computer-controlled self-levelling air springs and anti-roll bar. Continuous damping control with four adjustable settings. Servotronic speed-sensitive power-assisted rack-and-pinion steering. Ventilated carbon/ceramic cross-drilled disc brakes on all four wheels, with ABS.
DIMENSIONS: Length: 17ft 4.94in (5307mm). **Width:** 6ft 4.6in (1946mm). **Height:** 4ft 6.3in (1380mm). **Wheelbase:** 9ft 0.07in (2745mm).
PERFORMANCE & FUEL CONSUMPTION: 206mph, 0-60mph in 4.0 sec, 17mpg (627bhp model).
PRODUCTION TOTAL: 42,225 (estimated; all Continental GT and GTC).

Continental GT V8 S Coupé and Convertible, 2014-2018

A higher-performance version of the V8-engined Continental GT was announced at the Frankfurt Motor Show in autumn 2013, with the name of V8 S. Sales began in early 2014. Engine power was raised to 521bhp (528PS) and torque to 502lb ft (680Nm), and the eight-speed automatic was recalibrated to improve response. Suspension uprights, spring and damper rates were also revised, along with the anti-roll bars, and the suspension was lowered by 10mm – changes broadly similar to those made for the GT Speed models at the same time.

Cosmetic changes were also similar to those for the GT Speed models. The V8 S took on dark-tinted front and rear lights, which were popular and were added to the GT Speed models a year later. A gloss black grille and the bodykit of aerodynamic front splitter, side sills and rear diffuser were added, together with new open-spoke 20in wheels, red brake callipers and the option of a sports exhaust. Two-tone interiors became available, together with several other interior features. For 2016, the V8 S again shared most of the production changes of the W12-engined Continental GT.

MODELS: V8 S Coupé, V8 S Convertible.
ENGINE: 3993cc twin-turbocharged V8 with 521bhp.
TRANSMISSION: ZF eight-speed automatic. Four-wheel drive with Torsen centre differential.
SUSPENSION, STEERING & BRAKES: Front independent suspension with four-link double wishbones, computer-controlled self-levelling air springs and anti-roll bar. Rear independent suspension with trapezoidal multi-links, computer-controlled self-levelling air springs and anti-roll bar. Continuous damping control with four adjustable settings. Servotronic speed-sensitive power-assisted rack-and-pinion steering. Ventilated carbon/ceramic cross-drilled disc brakes on all four wheels, with ABS.
DIMENSIONS: Length: 17ft 4.94in (5307mm). **Width:** 6ft 4.6in (1946mm). **Height:** 4ft 6.3in (1380mm). **Wheelbase:** 9ft 0.07in (2745mm).
PERFORMANCE & FUEL CONSUMPTION: 192mph (GTC 190mph), 0-60mph in 4.4 sec, 26mpg.
PRODUCTION TOTAL: 42,225 (estimated; all Continental GT and GTC).

Continental GT3-R, 2014-2015

The GT3-R coupé released in late 2014 took its name from the Continental GT3 competition cars that had been successful in endurance racing events around the world during 2014. It had its origins in a skunkworks project which turned out so well that the car was approved for limited-volume production.

The GT3-R was based on the V8-powered Continental GT, with engine power raised to

572bhp and a shorter final drive to improve acceleration. This also resulted in a lower top speed. A tuned exhaust released some extra power and also provided a distinctive rumbling sound. Stiffened suspension was one element in the model's sharper handling, which also featured torque-vectoring for the first time in a Bentley, where the inside brake was automatically pulsed during high-speed cornering to help turn-in. Lighter materials and the omission of the rear seats saved 100kg, and these cars had extra-large carbon-ceramic brakes.

MODEL: Coupé.
ENGINE: 3993cc twin-turbocharged V8 with 572bhp.
TRANSMISSION: ZF eight-speed automatic. Four-wheel drive with Torsen centre differential.
SUSPENSION, STEERING & BRAKES: Front independent suspension with four-link double wishbones, computer-controlled self-levelling air springs and anti-roll bar. Rear independent suspension with trapezoidal multi-links, computer-controlled self-levelling air springs and anti-roll bar. Continuous damping control with four adjustable settings. Servotronic speed-sensitive power-assisted rack-and-pinion steering. Ventilated carbon/ceramic cross-drilled disc brakes on all four wheels, with ABS and torque-vectoring.
DIMENSIONS: Length: 17ft 4.94in (5307mm). **Width:** 6ft 4.6in (1946mm). **Height:** 4ft 6.3in (1380mm). **Wheelbase:** 9ft 0.07in (2745mm).
PERFORMANCE & FUEL CONSUMPTION: 170mph, 0-60mph in 3.7 sec, 22mpg.
PRODUCTION TOTAL: 300.

Continental Supersports, 2017-2018

The final development of the W12-engined Continental GT was the Supersports model, which delivered even greater performance from an engine that now had 700bhp (710PS) with 750lb ft (1017Nm) of torque. The standard wheels were 21in, with silicon carbide brake discs, and the suspension was lowered and stiffened. There was also a further-developed version of the torque-vectoring system used on the Continental GT3-R.

Supersports models had the bodykit of aerodynamic front splitter, side sills and rear diffuser, together with carbon fibre bonnet vents and gloss black for the wing vents and tailpipe, and a black finish for the exterior brightwork. The wheels were black with bright machined highlights, and Supersports side decals were an option. New for the interior were three-colour options, with diamond-quilted upholstery and Alcantara door trims. The Supersports name was embroidered on the seats and there were other interior features unique to the model.

On top of this, an optional X Specification brought a series of special paint finishes, carbon fibre trim items and wheels with an all-over gloss black finish.

MODELS: Supersports Coupé, Supersports Convertible.
ENGINE: 5998cc W12 with 700bhp.
TRANSMISSION: ZF eight-speed 8HP incorporating 'Quickshift' mode. Four-wheel drive with Torsen centre differential.
SUSPENSION, STEERING & BRAKES: Front independent suspension with four-link double wishbones, computer-controlled self-levelling air springs and anti-roll bar. Rear independent suspension with trapezoidal multi-links, computer-controlled self-levelling air springs and anti-roll bar. Continuous damping control with four adjustable settings. Servotronic speed-sensitive power-assisted rack-and-pinion steering. Enlarged ventilated carbon/ceramic cross-drilled disc brakes on all four wheels, with ABS.
DIMENSIONS: Length: 17ft 4.94in (5307mm). **Width:** 6ft 4.6in (1946mm). **Height:** 4ft 6.3in (1380mm). **Wheelbase:** 9ft 0.07in (2745mm).
PERFORMANCE & FUEL CONSUMPTION: 209mph, 0-60mph in 3.4 sec, 17mpg.
PRODUCTION TOTAL: 710.

Pictured on the famous Goodwood circuit, this 2017 Supersports has the optional side identification decal.

THE OTHER VOLKSWAGEN BENTLEYS

The high-performance Continental GT models established the new Bentley range at the start of the new century, but the plan was always to follow up as soon as possible with a new four-door saloon model. In the meantime, the Arnage remained in production to hold Bentley's place in the market.

Continental Flying Spur, 2005-2013

The first of the new Bentley saloons was announced at the Geneva Motor Show in 2005 and took the name of Continental Flying Spur. This name had been coined for the four-door sports saloon by H J Mulliner on the Bentley S Type Continental chassis of the late 1950s and early 1960s, and the decision to resurrect it deliberately hinted that the new saloon also had a sporting side. In practice, the new Flying Spur would add a sporting dimension to the saloon range that even the higher-performance derivatives of the Arnage had been unable to provide.

The new saloon was built on an extended version of the Continental GT underframe, with its wheelbase increased by 319mm, or about 12.6in, to provide room for a full-size passenger compartment. There were also a number of revisions to the steering, including a new steering rack and steering column, and alterations to other components to suit.

Demand for the GT was already so great that the production capacity at Crewe originally intended for the Flying Spur had been consumed. As a result, production was relocated to the Volkswagen plant in Dresden, Germany, alongside the slow-selling VW Phaeton to which the new Bentley was distantly related. Only when pressure eased did production switch completely to Crewe, in October 2006, by which time quite a large number of Flying Spurs had been built. The first Flying Spurs – all destined for European buyers – thus became the first (and only) Bentleys not to be assembled in the UK, although all their key components were built at Crewe.

Early cars were criticised for road, wind and suspension noise and, as production proceeded, Bentley gradually addressed these shortcomings. For the 2007 season, the satnav system was improved (as on other models at the time) and a new 19in five-spoke road wheel was introduced, which could be chromed at extra cost. The bespoke options were increased and a Mulliner driving specification became available, bringing 20in two-piece wheels, diamond-quilted leather and other special interior features. For 2008, the Flying Spur took on a more upright grille and larger lower air intakes, plus bright tail lamp bezels, a black rear valance and a slimmer rear bumper with wraparound brightware.

In the 2008 season, the Flying Spur range was broadened with the addition of a Speed model. This came with the 600bhp W12 engine introduced a year earlier in the Continental GT Speed, and had a lower ride height, ceramic brake discs and sharper steering. Visual distinction came from 20in

The front of the Flying Spur deliberately resembled that of the Continental GT, to provide a family resemblance.

There were similarities at the rear, too, although the 'haunches' were not carried over from the coupé.

Interior fittings were in line with the expectations of Bentley saloon customers.

The Flying Spur Speed added extra performance into the equation. This is it at the 2010 Geneva Show.

wheels, dark-tinted radiator and air intake grilles and wider, 'rifled' exhaust tailpipes. Upholstery was diamond-quilted, and the sound insulation was improved.

The later production history of these cars was characterised by several limited editions. April 2010 brought a Continental Flying Spur Speed China, as a companion to the Continental GT Design Series China edition. Revised to suit Chinese tastes, these cars had a new comfort suspension setting and a quieter exhaust. China had become the second largest market for the Flying Spur, and in September 2011 received a second special edition, this time of ten cars with wood interior trim by the British design company Linley, which had been founded in 1985 by David Linley, nephew of the queen.

The Middle East, which by that stage accounted for 10 per cent of all Bentley sales worldwide, received Flying Spur Arabia models in autumn 2010, available as both standard and Speed types. For other markets, the Series 51 upgrades were announced in November 2010, although deliveries did not begin until March 2011. The Series 51 cars featured 19in nine-spoke alloy wheels with a graphite finish, and new blue brake callipers visible through them. They also gained front wing vents, further interior upgrades and a new range of two-tone paint options.

Special interior wood treatments were a feature of the Flying Spur Linley.

MODELS: Continental Flying Spur, Continental Flying Spur Speed.
ENGINE: 5998cc twin-turbocharged W12 with 552bhp or 600bhp (Speed model).
TRANSMISSION: ZF 6HP26 automatic. Four-wheel drive with Torsen centre differential.
SUSPENSION, STEERING & BRAKES: Front independent suspension with four-link double wishbones, computer-controlled self-levelling air springs and anti-roll bar. Rear independent suspension with trapezoidal multi-links, computer-controlled self-levelling air springs and anti-roll bar. Continuous damping control with four adjustable settings. Servotronic speed-sensitive power-assisted rack-and-pinion steering. Ventilated disc brakes on all four wheels, with ABS.
DIMENSIONS: Length: 17ft 4.94in (5307mm), 17ft 4.3in (5290mm) from 2009. **Width:** 6ft 11.39in (2118mm) over mirrors. **Height:** 4ft 10.2in (1479mm). **Wheelbase:** 10ft 0.7in (3065mm).
PERFORMANCE & FUEL CONSUMPTION: 195mph, 0-60mph in 4.9sec, 17mpg (standard saloon), 200mph, 0-60mph in 4.5 sec, 17mpg (Speed model).
PRODUCTION TOTAL: 17,973 (unverified).

The Azure convertible had the difficult task of replacing the earlier car of the same name.

Azure, 2006-2010

The second-generation Bentley Azure convertible was intended as one of a pair of two-door models based on the Arnage platform, the other being the coupé that became the Brooklands. The wheelbase size and the body forward of the windscreen remained unchanged from the parent car, but there were major reinforcements to the underbody, the sills and the A-pillars, as well as to the rear subframe. The result was a bodyshell that was 300 per cent stiffer than that of the previous Azure that had gone out of production in mid-2003.

The new car was first presented as a concept at the January 2005 Los Angeles Motor Show, with the name of Arnage Drophead Coupé, and the production model then appeared at the Frankfurt Motor Show that September. Deliveries began in spring 2006, when the car cost twice as much as a Continental GT, but was also less expensive than the last of the earlier Azure convertibles.

The two primary influences on the shape were the earlier Azure and the 1955 Park Ward drop-head coupé on the Bentley S Type chassis. The windscreen was shallower and more steeply raked than on the Arnage, and the triple-layer convertible top stowed away completely out of sight. There was full automation of raising and lowering, and rollover hoops popped up automatically from behind the rear headrests if sensors detected that the car was about to turn over. On the inside, the dashboard was essentially the same as in the Arnage.

The first cars were built with the same BMW twin-turbo V8 engine and four-speed gearbox as the contemporary Arnage saloon, but Volkswagen did not wish to continue buying engines from a rival manufacturer and therefore prepared an updated version of the older 6.75-litre V8 for the 2007 and later cars. This had twin low-inertia turbochargers, and drove through a ZF six-speed gearbox.

In November 2008, the Azure T was announced at the Los Angeles Auto Show, with a focus on performance enhancements. This had the 500PS version of the 6.75-litre twin-turbo V8, giving 11 per cent more power than the standard Azure. It also incorporated the full range of electronic driver aids pioneered on the companion Brooklands coupé. The Azure T came with several distinguishing features. These included 'Le Mans' air vents low down on the front wings, and a body-colour grille surround with dark-tinted upper and lower

There was once again a deliberate family resemblance at the rear, but the Azure had its own special elegance.

The lines of the Azure worked well from every angle. The tight-fitting top is seen to advantage here.

With the convertible top in place, the Azure retained its sleek lines.

The Azure dash was quite different from that of the Flying Spur, yet clearly from the same school of thought.

grilles, exactly as on the Brooklands coupé. In addition, there were 20in two-piece alloy wheels with a five-spoke design, and some special interior features. The last Azure models of all types were built in 2010, and the car had no immediate successor.

MODELS: Azure, Azure T.
ENGINE: 6750cc twin-turbocharged V8 with 450PS (standard) or 500PS (Azure T).
TRANSMISSION: Four-speed GM 4L80-E automatic gearbox (2006 models), six-speed ZF 6HP26 automatic gearbox (2007 and later models).
SUSPENSION, STEERING & BRAKES: Independent front suspension with coil springs, twin wishbones, anti-roll bar and electro-hydraulic dampers. Independent rear suspension with coil springs, twin wishbones, anti-roll bar and electro-hydraulic dampers. Power-assisted rack-and-pinion steering. Ventilated disc brakes on all four wheels, lightweight carbon and silicon carbide discs optional on Azure T.
DIMENSIONS: Length: 17ft 8.2in (5389mm). **Width:** 6ft 2.8in (1900mm), 6ft 11.7in (2125mm) over mirrors. **Height:** 4ft 10.7in (1491mm). **Wheelbase:** 10ft 2.6in (3116mm).

PERFORMANCE & FUEL CONSUMPTION: 171mph, 0-60mph in 5.9 sec, 14.5mpg (standard model), 179mph, 0-60mph in 5.2 sec, 14.5mpg (Azure T).
PRODUCTION TOTAL: 1321.

The Azure T was the performance model, readily distinguished by its wheels and wing vents.

The Brooklands coupé successfully combined presence with the suggestion of great power.

Brooklands, 2008-2011

The coupé version of the two-door models based on the Arnage platform was announced as the Bentley Brooklands at the Geneva Show in March 2008. From the beginning, this model was designed as the Bentley flagship, and to ensure its exclusivity, production was limited to 550 examples. By the time of the show, the first 500 had already been spoken for.

Bentley was very proud of the 'floating' rear screen on the Brooklands coupé.

The turbocharged 6.75-litre V8 engine in the Brooklands was signed by the craftsman who built it.

The lines of the lower body followed those seen on the Azure convertible, but the Brooklands coupé was more than just a fixed-roof version of the same shell. Its roof incorporated what Bentley called a 'floating' rear screen located some way above the edge of the boot lid to achieve a more flowing line – a design that could not be mass-produced but required the rear wings to be hand-welded to the body pillars.

The car came with 'Le Mans' air vents low down on the front wings, with a dark-tinted grille matrix, and with a 'jewelled' fuel filler cap made from aluminium billet. It had two large-diameter oval tailpipe finishers and special 20in alloy wheels with a 16-spoke design. A five-spoke, two-piece sports style was available as an alternative.

Brooklands coupés had a special 530PS hand-built version of the 6.75-litre V8 engine, developed from the 500PS derivative in the Arnage T with a new air induction system, altered valve timing and a recalibrated management system. The Mitsubishi turbochargers were also new, and the sports exhaust system was tuned to give a distinctive roar under acceleration. The gearbox was a ZF six-speed, the extra body stiffness that the roof provided permitted changes to the Azure suspension that improved the ride, and there was the usual array of sophisticated electronic systems to assist the driver.

Among the multiple catalogued options for the Brooklands was the lightweight braking system introduced on the Continental

Bentley's distinctive diamond-quilted upholstery was a feature of the Brooklands.

GT Diamond Series in 2006. The Mulliner personalisation scheme provided even more variety, with the result that it was highly unlikely that any two cars were built to exactly the same specification.

The end of Brooklands production in 2011 also marked the end of Bentley production based on platforms designed under the old Rolls-Royce regime at Crewe.

MODEL: Coupé.
ENGINE: 6750cc twin-turbocharged V8 with 530PS.
TRANSMISSION: Six-speed ZF 6HP26 automatic gearbox.
SUSPENSION, STEERING & BRAKES: Independent front suspension with coil springs, twin wishbones, anti-roll bar and electro-hydraulic dampers. Independent rear suspension with coil springs, twin wishbones, anti-roll bar and electro-hydraulic dampers. Power-assisted rack-and-pinion steering. Ventilated disc brakes on all four wheels, lightweight carbon discs optional.
DIMENSIONS: Length: 17ft 9.03in (5411mm). **Width:** 6ft 9.8in (2078mm) over mirrors. **Height:** 4ft 10in (1473mm). **Wheelbase:** 10ft 2.6in (3116mm).
PERFORMANCE & FUEL CONSUMPTION: 184mph, 0-60mph in 5.0 sec, 14.5mpg.
PRODUCTION TOTAL: 550.

The Mulsanne saloon featured its own front-end design with an unmistakeable light arrangement.

Mulsanne, 2010-2020

The 2010-model Mulsanne revived a name last used in 1992 and replaced the Arnage as the four-door Bentley saloon. The car was previewed in August 2009 at the Pebble Beach concours event in California, had its European launch at the Frankfurt Show in September, then a follow-up US launch at the January 2010 Detroit Show. First deliveries were made in September 2010.

The basis of the Mulsanne was a completely new rear-wheel-drive platform with air suspension. This had an electronic control system called continuous damping control (CDC) that automatically lowered the car at speed to improve aerodynamics and stability. Power came from an extensively redesigned twin-turbo 6.75-litre V8 engine, now with an aluminium alloy block instead of the original cast iron type, and the addition of cam phasing and a cylinder deactivation system. With 505bhp (512PS), this had a very wide torque band, and Bentley claimed overall

The rear view of the Mulsanne employed familiar styling cues, and added a more restrained version of the Continental GT's 'haunches'.

The dashboard of the Mulsanne featured a deliberately more formal style. The rear seats were designed as two separate armchairs, for maximum comfort.

improvements of 15 per cent in fuel economy and CO2 emissions.

The Mulsanne was longer and more spacious than the long-wheelbase derivatives of recent Bentley saloons. A long bonnet and very short front overhang gave the required impression of power, and a kick-up in the body crease towards the rear gave the car the muscular 'haunches' that recalled those on the Continental GT. The nose echoed the Bentley style already established under Volkswagen, with twin circular light units flanking the classic mesh grille with its body-colour surround. Notably, the outer headlamps were mounted some way below the inner pair. At the rear were 'floating' elliptical light clusters, and the rear screen was enveloped in the body sheet metal to give the same sort of flowing line Bentley had achieved for the Brooklands coupé. The wheels were 20in alloys, and there were two 21in options, one of them a two-piece type.

The bodyshell used high-strength steel and aluminium, with superformed alloy panels to reduce weight. The boot lid was made of a composite polymer, and the radio aerial was embedded in it. Keyless entry and acoustic glazing were standard, and the seats were upholstered with leather that had been tanned traditionally to provide the right smell. The rear seats were power-adjustable, and there were comfort, premier and entertainment option packages. The Mulliner driving specification added 21in wheels, a sports suspension and other items.

Over time, the Mulsanne range was expanded through Speed and long-wheelbase models. The Speed model arrived first, in 2014, with a 530bhp version of the 6.75-litre engine that featured a redesigned combustion system. The suspension had a selectable sports setting, and the wheels and tyres were the first directional types used on a Bentley. Exterior features included a dark tint finish for the matrix

The 6.75 Edition of the Mulsanne commemorated final production of the 6.75-litre V8.

grille, special headlights and rifled exhaust tailpipes.

The long-wheelbase car was introduced at the Geneva Show in 2016 and was called the Mulsanne Extended Wheelbase. It was 10in (250mm) longer than the standard car, and among its features were a sunroof for the rear compartment and the option of electronically operated leg rests for the rear-seat passengers.

At the Moscow motor show in 2012, a Mulliner executive interior option was introduced with alternative theatre or iPad specifications. The 2016 Geneva launch of the Extended Wheelbase model also brought a Mulliner Grand Limousine version that was extended by 39in (or one metre). Always intended as a very limited production model, this had two additional rearward-facing seats. Each seat was individually air-conditioned, and there was an electrochromic glass division to separate the passengers from the driving compartment.

From 2012, there were several special editions of the Mulsanne, and these are discussed separately below. There were also two concept cars that explored possible design directions. The first was the Executive Interior Concept, which was displayed at the Los Angeles Show in 2011 and focused on multimedia connectivity, and the second was the Grand Convertible Concept, a four-seat convertible shown in Los Angeles in 2014 and widely supposed to be a replacement for the Azure.

The last Mulsanne models were part of a run-out edition called the 6.75 Edition by Mulliner, described in more detail below. The very last car was built in June 2020, and had the additional distinction of being the final car to have the 6750cc V8 engine, which was then withdrawn because it could not be updated to meet planned new emissions regulations. The Mulsanne model was not directly replaced, and a new generation of the Flying Spur filled its place in the Bentley range.

MODELS: Mulsanne, Mulsanne Speed, Mulsanne Extended Wheelbase, Mulsanne Mulliner Grand Limousine, Special editions (see below).
ENGINE: 6750cc twin-turbocharged V8 with 512PS, 530bhp for Speed models.
TRANSMISSION: Eight-speed ZF 8HP automatic gearbox. Four-wheel drive with Torsen centre differential.
SUSPENSION, STEERING & BRAKES: Independent front suspension with double wishbones, electronically controlled air springs and automatic ride height control. Independent multi-link rear suspension with electronically controlled air springs and automatic ride height control. Servotronic speed-sensitive power-assisted rack-and-pinion steering. Two-piece disc brakes on all four wheels; electronic parking brake; ABS.
DIMENSIONS: Length: 219.49in (5575mm). **Width:** 75.8in (1926mm) with mirrors folded. **Height:** 4ft 11.88in (1521mm). **Wheelbase:** 128.6in (3266mm).
PERFORMANCE & FUEL CONSUMPTION: 186mph, 0-60mph in 5.1 sec, 14-15mpg (standard saloon), 190mph, 0-60mph in 4.8 sec, 14-15mpg (Speed model).
PRODUCTION TOTAL: 7929.

Mulsanne Special Editions, 2012-2020

There were several special editions of the Mulsanne, as follows.

Diamond Jubilee Edition, 2012

This edition of 60 cars was introduced at the Beijing Motor Show and celebrated the Diamond Jubilee of Queen Elizabeth II. Among its special features were an embroidered state coach logo on the headrests and scatter cushions.

The Diamond Jubilee Edition had specially embroidered interior features. (Eddy1/Flickr)

Two-colour paintwork was an attractive feature of the Birkin Mulsanne.

Le Mans Edition, 2013

This was a US market edition introduced at the Pebble Beach concours event in 2013 which went on sale in the third quarter of the year. It was released at the same time as the Continental GT Le Mans edition, and Bentley promised a total of 288 cars, split between the two types. There were six different versions, each named after one of the Bentley drivers who took the cars to victory at Le Mans between 1924 and 2003: John Duff, Dudley Benjafield, Woolf Barnato, Tim Birkin, Glen Kidston and Guy Smith. All these cars had special exterior colour schemes and interior features.

The Mulsanne Shaheen was a special edition for the Middle East. (Abdullah AlBargan)

Shaheen Edition, 2013

This special edition was specific to the Middle East and was announced at the 2013 Dubai Motor Show. It was named after the shaheen (a peregrine falcon used in hunting) and came with the Mulliner driving specification as standard.

Seasons Collector's Editions, 2013

This was another special edition with multiple options, and in this case was created for China. There were ten cars for each of the four seasons, and a single Golden Pine car to represent the whole year. All of them had the Mulliner driving specification.

Birkin Edition, 2014

This was a special edition for Europe, named after the legendary Bentley racing driver Tim Birkin. There were 22 examples, each with the Mulliner driving specification, the entertainment package, and special 21in wheels. The cars came with a luggage set, numbered door sill plates, and the Bentley Flying-B logo embroidered on the headrests and inlaid on the wood trim. They were available in two-tone blue or in single-colour ghost white or damson.

Mulsanne 95 Edition, 2014

This edition of 15 cars for the UK celebrated Bentley's 95th anniversary as a marque. The cars were available in red, white or blue.

The Mulsanne 95 edition rang the changes on interior features.

Looking deliberately menacing, this is the Blue Train edition that was named after a legendary race.

Mulsanne Speed Blue Train Edition, 2015

This edition commemorated the occasion in 1930 when Bentley Chairman Woolf Barnato drove his Speed Six to race the famous Blue Train that ran from the south of France, and not only beat it but arrived in London before the train had reached Calais. He arrived four minutes before the train reached its destination, and to match that there were four examples of the Blue Train Edition. The car was introduced at the Techno-Classica car show in Essen, Germany, in April 2015, and the first example was supplied with a special matching picnic hamper. All four had a squared mesh grille, special dashboard features and door trims designed to recall the original Speed Six, and special treadplates reading 'Blue Train 85 Years'.

Mulsanne WO Edition, 2018

The WO Edition, named after marque founder W O Bentley, was introduced at the Geneva Show in 2018 and was a 100-strong limited edition that celebrated the marque's centenary (which was actually in 2019). Six cars had the Speed specification. All cars had two-tone paint and a chromed grille surround, and each one featured a piece of the crankshaft from an 8-litre Bentley, in a display case built into the armrest. Self-levelling wheel badges were among the special features.

6.75 Edition by Mulliner, 2020

The last 30 Mulsanne models built became a run-out edition called the 6.75 Edition after the 6.75-litre size of their V8 engines. The name was chosen because the engine was ending production at the same time, after a production run that had started 61 years

The huge bright-finish grille of the WO Edition recalled the days before painted shells took over. (Matti Blume, CC-SA 4.0)

earlier with its 6230cc naturally aspirated ancestor.

Flying Spur, 2013-2019

The Flying Spur saloon introduced at the Geneva Show in March 2013 had the job of replacing the Mulsanne and the earlier Flying Spur. To that end it was available with two engines: the 616bhp W12 and (from 2014) the 500bhp V8, both with twin turbochargers and cylinder deactivation systems, and both driving the rear wheels through a ZF eight-speed automatic gearbox. The car was no longer a Continental Flying Spur like its predecessor; the Continental name had been dropped to distance the luxury saloon from the sporting Continental GT. The first customer deliveries were made in August 2013.

The Flying Spur was built on the floorpan of the older car, although major changes, which were designed among other things to increase rigidity, made it almost completely new. The suspension was changed in detail to give a softer ride, but retained the adaptive damping system that could firm it up for sharper handling. The standard wheels were 19in, but 20in and 21in were also available.

Its key target markets were the US and China, with the latter expected to absorb up to 60 per cent of all cars built. The styling was designed to give the car both gravitas and presence, although at the same time the overall aim was to create a more ostentatious and extrovert car than before to suit tastes in its main markets. Every exterior panel was new, with sharp feature lines and a bold, angular version of the Bentley rear haunches and with a redesigned rear that incorporated trapezoidal tail lamp clusters. Weight was reduced through lighter materials, while comfort and sound insulation were improved, particularly for the rear-seat occupants, for whom power-adjustable individual seats were an option.

New technology included a hard disk for navigation and audio data and an optional twin screen entertainment system for rear-seat passengers. Audio and climate settings could be controlled by a wireless touchscreen controller or through an app on a paired device. Options gave customers the ability to create a more bespoke car than was possible with the earlier Flying Spur – an initiative that continued the direction set by the Mulsanne. The Mulliner specification brought diamond-quilted upholstery, chrome detailing, 21in wheels and other extras.

The range was expanded for 2016 with a pair of S models: the W12 S with engine power increased to 626bhp and a V8 S with 521bhp. Both cars had a more performance-focused suspension tune, and were distinguished visually by a different grille, gloss black window frames and door handles, and by a gloss black rear diffuser. The W12 S also had a unique grille. Inside, the headlining had a strip of contrasting colour and material down the centre. These cars came with a bench seat for three, but the twin power-adjustable seats of the standard W12-engined Flying Spur were available as an option, as were ceramic brake discs.

There was then a Black Edition of the V8 S for the 2018 season, announced in July 2017. Following the previous year's Continental GT Speed Black Edition, this had the chrome exterior trim blacked out. The wheels were 21in, uniquely in black, and were accompanied by black or, optionally red, brake callipers. The black theme was continued inside, where black leather with red contrast stitching was matched by piano black wood trim.

The last of these Flying Spur models were built in 2019, when a new model with the same name was released to replace them.

MODELS: Flying Spur, Flying Spur V8, Flying Spur W12 S, Flying Spur V8 S.
ENGINE: 5998cc twin-turbo W12 616bhp (625PS) or 626bhp (635PS) for W12 S, 3993cc twin-turbo V8 with 500bhp (507PS) or 521bhp (528PS) for V8 S.
TRANSMISSION: ZF 8HP automatic with 'Quickshift'. Four-wheel drive with Torsen centre differential.
SUSPENSION, STEERING & BRAKES: Front independent suspension with four-link double wishbones, computer-controlled self-levelling air springs and anti-roll bar. Rear independent suspension with trapezoidal multi-links, computer-controlled self-levelling air springs and anti-roll bar. Continuous damping control with adjustable settings. Servotronic speed-sensitive power-assisted rack-and-pinion steering. Ventilated disc brakes on all four wheels, with ABS.
DIMENSIONS: Length: 17ft 4.4in (5295mm). **Width:** 77.8in (1976mm), 87in (2208mm) over mirrors. **Height:** 58.6in (1488mm). **Wheelbase:** 10ft 0.7in (3065mm).
PERFORMANCE & FUEL CONSUMPTION: 199mph, 0-60mph in 4.3 sec, 19.2mpg (W12), 202mph, 0-62mph in 4.5 sec, 19mpg (W12 S), 183mph, 0-62mph in 5.2 sec, 25mpg (V8), 190mph, 0-62mph in 4.9 sec, 25.9mpg (V8 S).
PRODUCTION TOTAL: 17,931 (unverified).

Bentayga, 2016-2020

At a time when SUVs were in demand so widely, Bentley had no choice but to develop one, which was of course a new departure for the marque. They were entirely right to do so, because the new model rapidly became their best-selling product.

The new SUV was based on the Volkswagen

The Bentayga managed to look very much a part of the Bentley family, despite its SUV proportions. (DeFacto, CCA-SA 4.0)

The rear view of the Bentayga shows familiar Bentley styling cues. (DeFacto, CCA-SA 4.0)

Bentley's first diesel model was a Bentayga variant, although the only external clues were in the wheel design. (Vauxford, CCA-SA 4.0)

The diesel model also had its own design of exhaust tips, but the difference was a subtle one. (Vauxford, CCA-SA 4.0)

Group's MLB structure (the letters stand for Modularer Längsbaukasten or modular longitudinal platform) first seen in 2012 and subsequently shared by Audi, Porsche and Volkswagen models as well as Bentley. A concept version of the SUV was displayed at the Geneva Motor Show in March 2012 with the name of EXP 9F, but this was subsequently redesigned with more generic SUV proportions. The production car was then previewed at the September 2015 Frankfurt Show.

The name of Bentayga had already been revealed in January 2015, and came from the Roque Bentayga in Gran Canaria; it was also a portmanteau of Bentley and the Taiga snow forest. The original plan was to build the car at the VW Group plant in Bratislava, Slovakia, alongside other MLB models, and the first bodies were indeed built there. However, after negotiation with the British government, body manufacture was moved to the VW plant at Zwickau-Mosel in Germany and the vehicles were completed at Crewe in a new assembly facility.

The Bentayga became the first Bentley to get the latest version of the 600bhp twin-turbo W12 engine with cylinder deactivation. An eight-speed ZF automatic gearbox and permanent four-wheel drive were standard. The body design featured the characteristic Bentley 'haunches' and the car could be configured with four, five or seven seats, in the last case including two occasional types.

Bentley launched the car as a First Edition of 608 examples, that number matching the 608PS of the W12 engine. The company had predicted sales of 3500 for the 2016 season but, as all those cars were ordered before sales began, production was increased to meet demand, and the first year's sales figure was 5586.

Range expansion followed. For 2017, a 4.0-litre twin-turbo V8 diesel option became available, marking the first time any Bentley had been built with a diesel engine. This was distinguished by front wing badges and trapezoid exhaust outlets. A top-specification Bentayga Mulliner was also added. A 4.0-litre twin-turbo V8 petrol engine followed for 2018, and at the Geneva Show in March 2018, yet another new model was introduced, this time a V6 hybrid. This combined a turbocharged V6 petrol engine with an electric motor to minimise emissions and fuel consumption without major sacrifices to performance, and became available to customers in October 2019.

Somewhat inevitably, autumn 2019 also brought a Bentayga Speed model with the W12 engine for the 2020 model-year, and in June 2020 a second-generation Bentayga range was announced, ending the successful first era of Bentley's SUV.

MODELS: Bentayga, Bentayga V8, Bentayga Speed, Bentayga diesel.
ENGINES: 5950cc twin-turbo W12 with 600bhp (608PS) or 626bhp (635PS) for Speed, 3996cc twin-turbo V8 with 542bhp (550PS), 3956cc twin-turbo V8 diesel with 429bhp (435PS), 2984cc V6 turbo with Hybrid electric motors and 443bhp (449PS).
TRANSMISSION: ZF 8HP90 automatic. Four-wheel drive with Torsen centre differential.
SUSPENSION, STEERING & BRAKES: Front independent suspension with four-link double wishbones, computer-controlled self-levelling air springs and anti-roll bar. Rear independent suspension with trapezoidal multi-links, computer-controlled self-levelling air springs and anti-roll bar. Continuous damping control with four adjustable settings. Servotronic speed-sensitive power-assisted rack-and-pinion steering. Ventilated disc brakes on all four wheels, with ABS.
DIMENSIONS: Length: 202.4in (5141mm). **Width:** 78.7in (1998mm), 87.5in (2222mm) over mirrors. **Height:** 68.6in (1742mm). **Wheelbase:** 117.8in (2992mm).
PERFORMANCE & FUEL CONSUMPTION: 187mph, 0-60mph in 4.0 sec, 21mpg (W12), 190mph, 0-62mph in 3.9 sec, 22mpg (Speed), 180mph, 0-60mph in 4.4 sec, 23.5mpg (V8), 168mph, 0-60mph in 4.6 sec, 36mpg (V8 diesel).
PRODUCTION TOTAL: 23,781 (to end 2020).

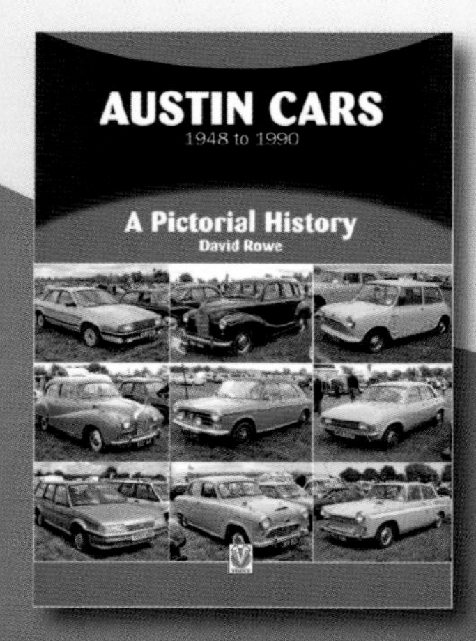

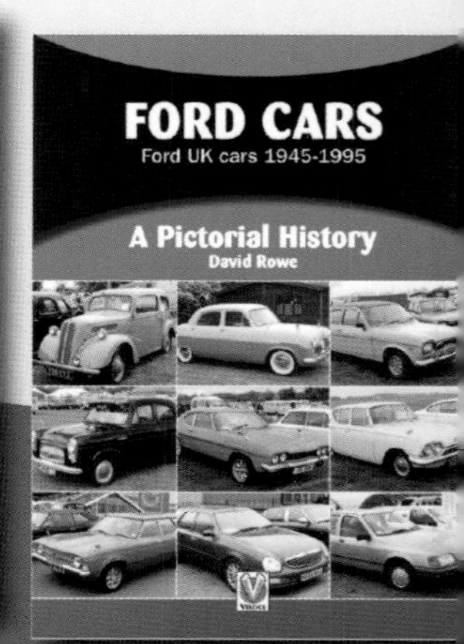

A Pictorial History – the series

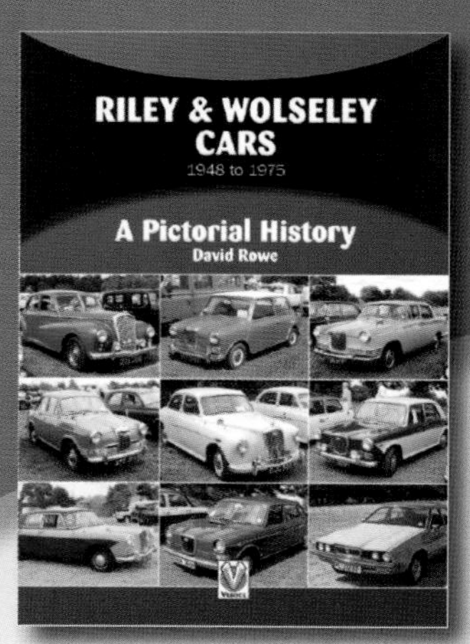

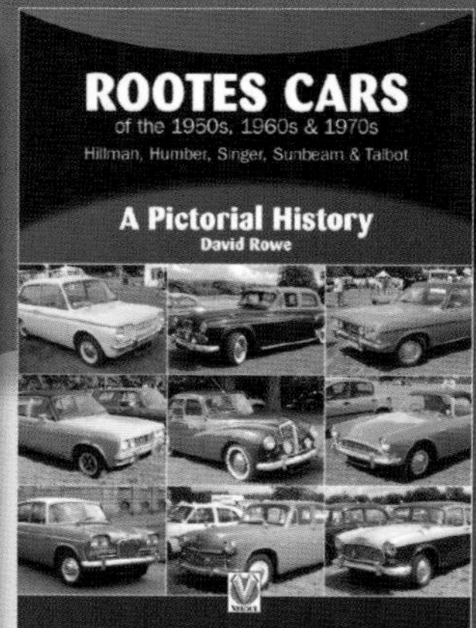

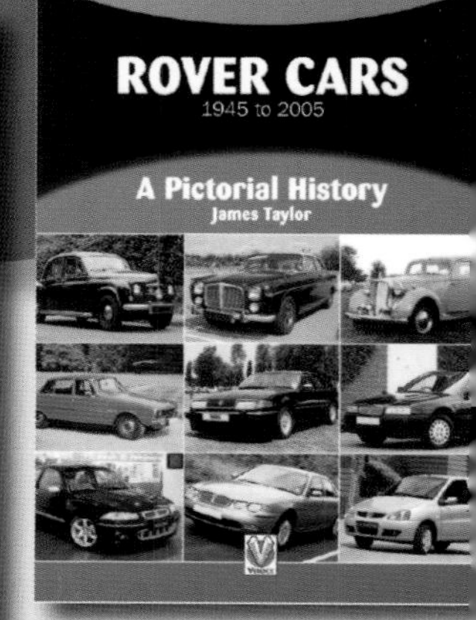

INDEX